Winning Them Over

How to Negotiate Successfully with Your Kids

Winning Them Over

How to Negotiate Successfully with Your Kids

Dr. Bradley Bucher
with William Proctor

𝔗𝔦𝔪𝔢𝔰 BOOKS

Published in the United States by Times Books, a division of Random House, Inc., New York, and simultaneously in Canada by Random House of Canada Limited, Toronto.

Library of Congress Cataloging-in-Publication Data

Bucher, Bradley D., 1932–
  Winning them over.

  Bibliography: p.
  1. Parent and child. 2. Intergenerational relations.
3. Negotiation. I. Proctor, William. II. Title.
HQ755.85.B83   1987   646.7'8   86–23172
ISBN 0–8129–1206–3

Designed by Mary Cregan
Manufactured in the United States of America

9 8 7 6 5 4 3 2

First Edition

To the parents, children, and colleagues who showed me my errors and helped me learn to correct them

Contents

Introduction   ix

1. Why Negotiate with Your Child?   3

2. The Secret to a Successful Negotiating Style   16

3. The Nuts and Bolts of Give-and-Take   41

4. Should You Put It in Writing?   74

5. How to Seal a Deal with the Token System   89

6. Back to the Bargaining Table   107

7. When Bargaining Breaks Down   132

8. Different Kids Need Different Deals   154

9. The Basic Facts of Civilized Life   169

10. The Great Goal of Self-Control   197

Selected Bibliography   205

Introduction

*A*s a parent, your most natural response to your children is to love, protect, and care for them. Second, you want to prepare them to enter the adult world with all the skills for living that you ever hoped or dreamed of possessing yourself.

The first of these heartfelt desires suggests a rich array of smiles, hugs, kisses, praises, treats, and privileges—and in general, an abundance of happiness. The second parental aim demands training. It's firmly rooted in schooling, moral education, training of practical abilities and social skills, self-control, foresight, alertness to responsibilities, wisdom, and judgment.

For many families, this second group of training objectives unfortunately often triggers negative reactions. As parents try to teach their offspring the basics of survival and success, they lapse into frowns, angry words, accusations, nagging, humiliating comments, demands, deprivation, and penalties. They may also resort to physical punishment, with all the negative reactions and emotions that can go with it.

The children, for their part, learn all too quickly how to return in kind the miseries that they have received. As a result, home becomes anything but the paradise parents may have dreamed of.

We do not promise a paradise in this book. But we do offer some ways for you to help your children grow and develop the skills that are important for success and happiness in life, with fewer of the negative interactions and more of the positive experiences that parents prefer. We'll try to show you how you can develop a more positive relationship with your children through the process of negotiation. At the same time, you'll be in a position to reap the pleasures that such a relationship can bring.

Parents may wonder if moral behavior can ever develop when parents restrict their training to positive methods. If children learn moral behavior through negotiation—and gain some advantage for being honest, truthful, or generous —won't they learn these behaviors are valuable mostly because of the rewards they bring?

Quite rightly, parents often feel that it's important for children to learn that ethical and moral patterns of behavior are worthy in themselves, without reference to any benefits these qualities may bring. For example, truthfulness should be valued independently of any gain to the speaker. Likewise, honesty and charity are usually valued most when they occur outside the view of those who might praise or condemn. Receiving rewards for these moral qualities might tempt a child to look primarily for the personal advantages that morally proper behavior will bring.

As compelling as this viewpoint may sometimes seem, I'm afraid I can't buy it. To respond, let me address an important assumption underlying this book. My experience as a child psychologist has convinced me that moral principles sturdy enough to resist strong temptations are not learned in an emotional vacuum. Parents who don't rely on rewards to train moral behaviors in their children will find that they must resort to coercion and punitive pressures when they detect violations of moral rules. What isn't taught by positive means must be taught by resort to threats and blame.

I see no clear advantage in teaching moral behavior primarily through pressure and punishment. Moral behavior learned through fear may eventually be cast aside when the dangers are past. Society arranges in many ways to make morally appropriate behavior beneficial for those who practice it. So punishment for violations should be the last, not the first, strategy to apply.

Consequently, this book will offer a positive approach— one that will, I think, produce adults whose morality will be lastingly built on love, not on fear.

—*Bradley D. Bucher, Ph.D.*

Winning Them Over

How to Negotiate Successfully with Your Kids

1.

Why Negotiate with Your Child?

*H*AVE you ever wished there could be a permanent peace treaty between you and your youngsters?

Imagine: No big arguments. No battles royal. No endless hassles over minor matters that can easily drive any adult to distraction.

In other words, imagine a relatively tranquil family atmosphere in which disputes are solved by reasonable discussions —with little waste of time and energy, and with all sides ending up satisfied.

Sound impossible? This result *is* impossible these days with many families, given the argumentative, confrontational habits they've developed. But peace and tranquillity are not only possible but probable when negotiation becomes the prevailing policy for solving problems with your children.

What exactly is involved in negotiating with kids? When we talk about negotiation, business or business-related activities come to mind. The very word *negotiation* comes from the Latin word *negotiari,* which means to carry on business. The major objective of negotiation in the hardheaded worlds of business, labor, and government is to set up a conference between two or more opposing—and often strong-willed—parties, and then to help them hammer out a settlement acceptable to all sides.

But as with many other useful concepts and techniques, negotiation has found important uses outside its original fields. In my specialty, psychology, the advantages of open, friendly interchange between parents and children are becoming increasingly clear. A child who speaks only when spoken to and who keeps his ideas to himself is likely not to be the caring and capable adult we would like him or her to become.

To show you what I mean, consider this scenario: "I lost my temper!" a single mother admitted tearfully to a therapist. "I got so mad that I hit him!"

Obviously this mother wasn't trying to hide anything. Things had gotten out of control at home, and she was no longer interested in putting up a brave front. She was desperate for help, and a therapist seemed to be her last hope.

The problem began when her son, Manny, a second-grader, refused to do his homework. They argued and argued, but day after day he went to school with no homework. What was Manny's problem? his mother wondered. Mainly, she had decided, he was just stubborn. In his mother's view, he had found a way to control his young life—*and* control his parent. He was pushing his newfound power for all it was worth. The mother's attitude of blaming her child for the problem was clearly laying the groundwork for more serious confrontation.

His teacher wasn't very sympathetic. She kept him in at recess to do his homework, while all the other children were outside playing. But even though Manny had to sit inside, this punishment did not change his behavior.

The teacher, who was becoming increasingly frustrated,

finally got in touch with Manny's mother and explained the situation. Every day, she said, Manny received a homework assignment that should have taken about twenty minutes to complete, but he hardly ever did it. It wasn't that he wasn't capable of doing it—his intelligence tests showed that he was. Besides, when he was kept in during recess to do it, he finished in short order.

Manny's teacher had embarrassed his mother by pointing out that it was important to train him to do his homework now, while he was young. In later years, she noted, the assignments would become longer and more difficult, and at that stage good work habits would be essential. The mother felt she was being blamed for not trying hard enough with Manny at home.

What followed was a nightly battle royal.

"You've got to do your homework *now!*"

"I won't!"

"Then you can't watch any more TV!"

"I don't care!"

One night the frustrated mother finally lost control. She picked up a bedroom slipper and whacked him with it. The frightened child, though he was not physically harmed, burst into tears. At this point the mother, alarmed by her action, decided to seek professional help. The next day she called and made an appointment to see the psychologist at the school.

During the conference that followed, the therapist discovered that the young mother was divorced and working at a full-time job. And besides eight-year-old Manny, there were two younger children in the family. But being saddled with sole responsibility for several young children wasn't the real source of the problem. When the woman came home from work, she looked forward to seeing her children, whom she dearly loved, and spending a pleasant, uncomplicated evening.

"My children have always come first with me," she declared. "I've tried to teach them that school is important. I just don't understand why Manny won't do his homework."

Yet the psychologist learned that Manny's mother really didn't have much free time to spend with him. Much of the time she did have was taken up with arguments. And both were left with bad feelings. As the mother got angry at inconsequential matters, Manny tended to avoid her.

When the therapist later asked Manny why he wouldn't do his homework, the eight-year-old would only reply, "I don't know. I don't want to do it. I don't like it."

So the therapist decided to ask the mother to try a new technique that was proving increasingly effective in such parent-child disputes. He suggested she attempt to negotiate with her son.

"Obviously," he explained, "Manny doesn't understand the importance of homework as well as you do. And it doesn't seem to help when you try to explain the situation to him, or nag, or argue. So what you need to do is 'make a deal' that will get the homework done *and* keep the peace."

In explaining the technique, he gave her the following list of suggestions for effective parent-child negotiation:

- Arrange a time when the two of you can be alone for a negotiating session, without interruptions.
- Let Manny know well in advance that you and he are going to get together for a talk.
- When the negotiation begins, be pleasant and stay calm. Try to keep things in perspective. After all, the world won't end tomorrow if Manny doesn't do his homework tonight!

- *Discuss* the basic problem: that he needs to keep up in school. There has to be give-and-take here; you can't just dictate solutions to him.
- Be prepared to offer some compensation to Manny that will be valuable enough to persuade him to do his homework. It probably won't have to be very much; but in any event, don't think in terms of punishment.

  A possible reward might be just for the two of you to do something enjoyable together when Manny gets his homework done. For example, you might play a game or read stories. Whatever you settle upon, you will probably find you'll have some good times together! Perhaps he would enjoy watching a TV show—*if* his homework is completed. Or maybe there's a special toy that he wants, and a system can be worked out for him to earn it by doing his homework.

  In other words, be ready to offer him a variety of choices. Also be sure to ask him what he wants. You may very well have overlooked his favorite activity or goal, so try to listen to him respectfully. At the very least, that will bring him into the negotiation and give him a chance to participate in the discussion.
- Be sure to keep the rewards realistic, since you do not want to agree to something that you cannot possibly do. And be certain you are in agreement about exactly what Manny has to do to get those rewards. Remember: Once you have made an agreement, you have to be sure what it is and be prepared to stick to it. Negotiation will not work unless your child can trust you.
- Always keep in mind two primary goals: (1) to get Manny to do his homework, and (2) to restore harmony in your relationship. And there's an important bonus: Part of your reward will be the increased affection and pleasure

Manny's achievement will inspire in you. Manny will certainly be happier, too.

The suggestions made sense to the harried mother, but making negotiation work at home involved more than just listing procedures on paper. When Manny's mother tried to get a discussion started, she had great difficulty getting the boy to talk. He didn't quite comprehend what was going on. And because of the angry emotional atmosphere that had existed, they both were quick to return to earlier unpleasant feelings. The mother tended to become irritated; Manny tended to withdraw. But at the same time, Mom may have surprised the boy and herself, too, because she was able to remain friendly and back away every time a confrontation seemed about to occur.

As Mom patiently offered various suggestions for rewards, Manny finally became interested. Eventually he decided to make an offer of his own. He suggested that he would do his homework immediately after school *if* he would be allowed to stay up later than his two younger siblings. He also wanted to have that extra time to play a favorite game with his mother. Apparently what Manny had wanted most all along was to have more of his mother's attention.

His misbehavior may even have intensified because of the attention his mother gave him. If so, the misbehavior worked. By acting up he could often induce his mother to sit down with him to help with his homework assignments. As too frequently happens with busy parents and teachers, Manny received more attention when he was being "bad" than when he was being "good." In such a case, a vicious cycle can be set in motion. When adults pay extra attention to a child who acts up, the wrong kind of behavior may be reinforced. In Manny's case, when his mother's attention and interaction were shifted to come *after* the work was done, the problem was quickly solved.

Manny's experience serves as a good illustration. Before negotiation took place, the best way he had to get the undivided attention of his busy mother was to make her dissatisfied with him. Similarly, in school the class was large, and he was able to spend some time alone with the teacher when he was being punished.

Negotiation, however, succeeded in breaking the cycle of misbehavior, and Manny's school problem ended as his mother stuck to their agreement.

This case is an example of how negotiation can be used in a "normal" family setting. There were no deep-seated problems with the child. Although there was no father in the home, the family was not extremely troubled. Of course I don't want anyone to think that parent-conducted negotiation can be a substitute for professional help when serious difficulties exist. But negotiation can be the key to dealing with many common problems that flare up in even the most loving families.

Before we go any further, however, let's consider in a little more detail what negotiation involves. As I've said, the first things that may come to mind are disputes between labor and management, or between countries. To avert outright conflict and perhaps disaster, both parties involved in the dispute meet to discuss and hammer out an acceptable agreement. Each interest group comes to these negotiating sessions knowing more or less what it wants and what it's prepared to give up in order to achieve important objectives. They then bargain until both feel that they have gained something important.

This is how genuine, effective negotiation operates. But what often takes place in business, politics, or families is quite different—what I call coerced agreements. These are grudg-ing, unsatisfying settlements that occur when one side uses its power to force the other side to give in.

For example, union members may threaten to strike at the moment when the company they work for has just received a big order. So, to keep the business, management agrees to meet the union's demands.

Or the reverse may take place. A company may refuse to negotiate a new contract with its employees when business is slow. In this case, management knows that the employees are probably afraid of losing their jobs. So the company ex-ploits the situation by driving an especially hard labor bar-gain.

Similar situations occur between countries. For example, one country may threaten war, or to ruin another's economy by withholding a vital resource, if certain demands are not met. The threatened country feels coerced to capitulate to the other's demands.

The uneasy settlements reached in these situations may keep the peace, at least temporarily. But these are not true negotiations since only one party is being satisfied. The pres-sures foster an atmosphere of anger and resentment that often leads to hostile outbursts against the overbearing party.

These same principles apply to relations between parents and children. Parents, because they are older, may know in a general way what's best for a child. But that doesn't mean the parent knows how to *communicate* what's best, or how to bring it about.

So the parent, perhaps feeling the pressures of a busy life, may *demand* a certain behavior from the child. When the child does not comply, the parent immediately, in knee-jerk fashion, lowers the boom with punishment or a threat of punishment.

If the child finally complies with the parent's demand under these circumstances, the youngster has entered into a coerced settlement. The parent may feel satisfied because the immediate goal has been accomplished. But the child will most likely harbor resentments that could begin to tick away like little time bombs.

Take the case of Manny. His mother first tried to get him to do his homework by nagging him and threatening to punish him if he didn't. She even resorted to physical force at one point. If he had done his homework in response to the threats, he would have entered into a coerced agreement with her. But the settlement would have been pleasing only to the mother—and their relationship would likely have deteriorated over the long haul.

Of course parents are not the only ones who misuse their power. Children may also attempt to exert some psychological pressure and force a settlement on Mom or Dad. For example, a young child who wants something his parents have said no to may throw a tantrum or whine until he gets it. Or children may sulk or nag until they get their own way. Many parents will give in because they can't tolerate their children's distress, or they want some harmony, peace, and quiet. They may convince themselves that if their child wants something so much, then the child must really *need* it —and they're justified in giving in.

A child learns very quickly the advantages of resorting to these unpleasant behaviors—especially if they have been successful in the past, or if he has seen his parents use them. Savvy youngsters also learn *when* to use coercion. Most parents do not want to create scenes when guests are present or when they are out shopping. Children, even very young ones, can take advantage of these adult feelings. So they often pick just the "best" time to make their demands. But this is not the sort of skill we want our children to master!

A major reason most parents—and children, for that matter—resort to coercion or threats is that they haven't learned they have a better alternative in negotiation. Parents of very young children may say, "I don't need to negotiate! I know how to get them to do what I want!" They are willing to tolerate their children's less troublesome misbehaviors because they know that adults usually have an advantage over their children in this power struggle. They can win the important battles, and for the minor skirmishes, giving in isn't really all that bad—at least, until the children reach their teenage years.

As children get older, however, the authoritarian parent will begin to feel his power to control his child's behavior slipping away. The children's peers become increasingly important, and the youngsters tend to become less dependent on the parents. Family battles intensify, and the child isn't so easy to defeat by threats and restraints. Consequently, I'm convinced that the earlier you can begin genuine negotiations with your child, the better.

For the majority of children, probably the youngest age that you can begin to negotiate meaningfully is four. A child has to be able to express his thoughts clearly in words before you can "horse trade" with him. But there is a wide variation in children's verbal abilities, and simple, on-the-spot negotiations can begin even earlier.

I once witnessed just such a simple negotiation between a father and his daughter, who was less than three years old. I had stopped by to visit an old college friend who had brought his family up from Florida to visit grandparents in the Northeast at Christmastime. As we sat in the cozy kitchen talking, we could hear my friend's little girl crying in her room upstairs. The youngster had been tucked into bed for the night, and usually, with very little coaxing, she would drift off into dreamland. But this time, even though the tot's grandmother went upstairs to try to soothe her to sleep, the child kept crying.

Finally my friend went upstairs and brought his sobbing daughter down to the kitchen. He sat the little child on his lap and said, "Stop crying and tell Daddy what's wrong. I can't help a little girl who is crying if she doesn't tell me what's wrong." To my amazement the toddler quickly pulled herself together, stopped crying, and answered, "Daddy, the sheets are cold!" Of course! She was from Florida and wasn't used to cold sheets.

My friend then proposed, "If I go upstairs and warm the sheets for you, will you promise to go to sleep?" The little girl readily agreed, and in a little while she was asleep.

Here, then, is an example of how fast, effective, and simple negotiation can be, even with a very young child. Such negotiation occurs in every family. But I was pleased that the girl expressed herself so well. Clearly, she was accustomed to having grown-up conversations with her father.

The point in this case is that you shouldn't underestimate your child's ability to reason and express his thoughts. If you just give him an opportunity, you may be surprised at what a rational turn your relationship with your youngster can take.

No matter what age your child is when you begin to negotiate, there are many important benefits that will immediately become apparent in your family relations. First of all, by providing a time for discussing problems between the two of you, you will help your child to develop his verbal skills. Children understand themselves and also their outside world better and better as they learn to describe their feelings, actions, and motivations in words. Moreover, being able to think, speak, and write accurately and logically are abilities that will be useful for the rest of the child's life.

During your negotiating sessions you'll get to know your child better; you'll learn more about what's going on in his or her life. Many times adults don't really listen to their children. Some parents think they're too busy to bother at those moments when their youngsters want to tell them something. So they put the children off, and thereby miss opportunities that may never occur again.

Getting into the habit of negotiating takes care of this problem. By setting aside times for talking together, you'll open the way to understanding your children better, and they'll understand themselves and you more completely.

Consider again Manny's case. His mother didn't realize the power of paying attention to her son until she began negotiating with him to get him to do his homework. Or take the case of my friend from Florida. He could have completely misinterpreted his daughter's crying if he hadn't taken a moment to discuss the problem with her.

Perhaps most important of all, negotiating with your children will foster more harmony, love, and happiness in the home. Parents and children will simultaneously develop a better understanding of the uses and misuses of power and control in the home. In the process they will use their influence more generously, and they will learn to respect and take pleasure in fulfilling each other's desires.

Clearly there are a number of benefits to negotiation. To enjoy them in practice in your own home, however, there are certain principles you must learn and certain bargaining skills you must master. To this end, as we explore the practical implications of negotiating with children in the following pages, you'll learn how to:

- Use the practical psychological tactics of negotiation to help children learn to respect others and achieve their full potential in life
- Talk persuasively with your children and develop powers of persuasion in them as well
- Take the pain and strain out of parent-child encounters
- Draft effective written agreements between you and your children
- Select the most effective negotiating tactics for children of different ages
- Minimize coercion, nagging, punishment, anger, and other negative feelings and interactions
- Help kids to mature more quickly
- Improve parent-child communications
- Enhance the moral development of both your child and yourself
- Eliminate tantrums and sulking
- Help older kids become more rational in their approach to their responsibilities and their relationships with others
- Learn what to do when agreements fail

Now let's consider the first step in effective family negotiation—the secret to a persuasive parental style.

2.

The Secret to a Successful Negotiating Style

*N*EGOTIATION is not always an easy skill to apply, especially if you've been in the habit of managing your children by relying on threats and commands. Like every new skill, negotiation requires learning unfamiliar, strange concepts. And if you want to become a truly expert negotiator, you'll probably have to *un*learn some old bad habits.

Let's now assume you want to create lasting settlements with your children, rather than impose shorter-term arrangements. You want to be persuasive, but you don't want to be coercive. How do you go about it?

The secret to having such a persuasive parental style in negotiating with children can be summed up very simply— be *positive*. To be a successful negotiator in parent-child interactions, you have to act positive and think positive. Among other things, this means choosing the reaction or response that reinforces positive rather than negative behavior.

Unfortunately many parents—even though they may *think* they are loving and positive—can sometimes be quite negative with their children. Think about it for a moment. You ask your boy to do something. He ignores you. You ask again. He continues to ignore you. The other pressures of the day have been gnawing away at you, and this is one too many. So you ask him once again, but quite sharply this time. He finally responds, but not by doing what you asked. He begins to argue or just says, in effect, "No, I don't want to!" So now what do you do? After things have gone this far, you're not likely to be positive!

When all else fails, the bottom line for many parents in dealing with their children tends to be a big minus. They issue a series of requests or orders. When these don't work, they move on to the loud, harsh voice, the threats, and the tears. Then they give up—or they drop the ax. Such an approach is coercion, not persuasion. It's an approach based on power, guilt, and penalties—not on cooperation, reason, and mutuality.

The older children get, and the more independent of their parents they become, the less effective a negative, strong-arm strategy proves to be. In fact, at any age, according to various psychological studies, the coercive way can have some very undesirable side effects. Children confronted with threats and negative consequences tend to bridle, drag their heels, or rebel outright.

In my own clinical experience, I've seen how negative elements sabotage prospects for agreement between parents and children. Negative factors may produce immediate results, but they will almost always militate against long-term peace in the household. Even a *hint* of negativism by the parent can cause attempts at a truly negotiated settlement to fail, especially if the child has learned to react with counter-measures against what he sees as coercion.

For example, I've seen the prospects for a valid negotiation break down when:

• *The parent promises a negative result if the child continues his undesirable behavior.* You know the typical scenario: "If you don't set the table right now, you're going to catch it!" Or, "If you don't finish your piano lesson, you won't be watching television tonight!"

The child may rebel and test your determination. Or he may comply, and look for ways to get back at you later. Such outcomes are far from satisfactory.

• *Parents use negative pressures to try to coerce cooperation.* These negative components may not be so easy to detect. But your child may tell you, "Mom, you're always nagging me." Perhaps Mom doesn't realize she has adopted such a negative tactic. Or perhaps she has learned from experience that unpleasant as nagging is, it seems in the end to be working. Also, a few sarcastic remarks and innuendos may be a help. So she responds, "I'll stop criticizing you and nagging when you do your chores." Meaning: "Until then, your life will be very unpleasant!"

These are logical, time-honored approaches to getting a youngster off dead center, aren't they? Yet such tactics don't work very well. They are quick and they provide a Band-Aid solution when encounters with children are particularly stormy and unmanageable. Ultimately, though, these approaches are poisonous. They poison your daily interactions with your children, and they'll poison any attempt at negotiations as well.

Although negotiating with such negative components as nagging and threats of punishment can lead into dangerous waters, too often the short-term benefit to the parents—the compliance, however reluctant—takes charge. The parents build up an arsenal of weapons against their child. Before long the child learns to turn those very weapons back against Mom and Dad—and perhaps, in later years, against his or her own children as well.

The first rule in mastering a persuasive parental style is to learn how to assume a *completely* positive approach. But isn't this only a dream? Can anyone be completely positive, especially when trying to deal with a rambunctious schoolchild? Besides, can being completely positive really work? When you've learned better how to use positive approaches, you'll begin to see how far they go.

There's no question that a totally positive approach to dealing with your children isn't easy. The Principles of Positive Parental Persuasion that we'll be presenting later in this chapter are not going to be as easy to apply as they are to read. The positive approach is particularly difficult at first, when you're trying to alter embedded negative habits in yourself and your child—habits that may have taken years to develop. But as you become more skillful, you'll begin to experience some of the results of a positive approach. Then you'll be more likely to become convinced.

That's what happened, quite by accident, to Phyllis, an elementary-school guidance counselor. Phyllis is now widely respected in her district for being able to handle difficult children of all ages, but that wasn't always the case. "I began my career as a third-grade classroom teacher in a poor, crowded urban area," Phyllis recalled. "There were many discipline problems in my class, and when they got too much for me to handle, I followed the standard procedure: I sent the offending child to the principal's office. Naturally, I expected the child to be punished. But to my growing irritation, that was not what usually happened."

Instead, after being taken to the office and remaining with the principal for a short time, the offender would return smiling happily. He'd had a talk with the principal, but he didn't seem to have been chastised by it. The child would walk up to Phyllis, hand her a written apology, and then promise to be better behaved in the future.

Phyllis didn't want to rock the boat with the school administration, so she would nod and tell the child to take his seat. But she always felt dissatisfied, as though justice had not quite been done. In short, what she really wanted was for some clear *punishment* to take place. She feared the child was actually profiting from his misbehavior.

As Phyllis settled in to the demands of her job and became better acquainted with her colleagues, she occasionally discussed the discipline situation with them. It soon became apparent that many of the others were dissatisfied, too. In general they were unhappy with the principal's methods because most felt that children should be "straightened out" severely for being disobedient. Despite the teachers' feelings, however, the school ran smoothly. Against all expectations, the staff got along well with each other and with the children. The children's parents were practically ecstatic over the educational progress that was being made.

"I began to think hard about how our principal handled not only children but adults as well," Phyllis reflected. "I noticed that somehow he was able to get me to do things I had no intention of doing at first. For instance," she explained, "I found myself attending a music workshop on my own time—even though I can neither carry a tune nor play an instrument! I was going simply because he had asked me to go—and surprisingly I didn't feel the least bit resentful. When I analyzed how this had come about, I began to understand and appreciate his technique."

It seems that the principal had first called her into his office and spoken to her graciously, praising her teaching ability and professional growth. Then he had asked her to think about attending the music workshop. When she protested because of her lack of musical ability, he suggested that she not limit herself personally or professionally. He also offered the carrot of glowing recommendations and a fine career in education if she took advantage of the opportunities presented to her.

Phyllis not only wound up agreeing with him; she actually felt good about the additional training!

Clearly, here was a man who was skillful in managing people, whether young or old. And his secret lay in being completely positive in his relationships and requests. He avoided throwing his weight around—a heavy-handed approach he could easily have taken as a school principal. He instead projected a nonthreatening, upbeat style, and the results at his school spoke for themselves.

The principal handled children in much the same way he handled adults. He talked to them quietly about their problems, and he gave them time to think about how much happier their life in school might be. He also offered suggestions as to what he thought more correct behavior should be.

In almost every case, the principal and the child would reach an agreement. He made sure to send the child off pleased and happy. This pleasant end to the negotiation was not a reward for misbehavior; in fact, for almost all of the children it was a reward for agreeing in a grown-up manner about the best way for a child to behave.

"When I thought about it, I realized that most of the time

his approach worked," said Phyllis. "So I decided to give it a try myself." For one thing, she stopped thinking about how to punish the children. Instead she concentrated her energies on getting the youngsters to act appropriately through discussions and the use of rewards for good behavior. She always used her principal's methods as her guide. "Once I began to pursue that line of thinking, I started to understand my students better, and my job became much easier," Phyllis recalled.

Parents will also find that the job of child-rearing becomes much easier if they shift to a more positive persuasive style. But how, in practical terms, do you achieve this?

It's not easy to stop thinking in terms of punishment. When parents are having trouble with their children, often their first reaction is to reach for sanctions such as spankings or taking away privileges. But such an attitude creates as many problems as it solves. Study after study in psychological clinics demonstrates dozens of ways punishment can go wrong.

So get the concepts of sanctions and retribution out of your mind and vocabulary, at least for now. To be sure, there's still a place for a heavier hand when negotiation breaks down, as we'll see in a later chapter. But for the present, just forget punishment and coercion! Instead, think about more positive tactics.

There's one main goal in every difficult encounter with your youngster: to get your child to change his behavior in some way for the better. In the last analysis, you're not really interested in exacting a pound of flesh for what has taken place in the past. Your main concern is the future. You're trying to help your children grow up to be the best people they can be. You also want to provide yourself with as happy a home life as possible.

This brings us to the Principles of Positive Persuasion that you need to learn and practice in order to carry out and conclude a successful negotiation.

Principle of Positive Persuasion 1.
Keep a positive attitude.

To achieve the most positive attitude, you should monitor yourself. You want to be sure that you're always projecting four essential qualities—which might be called the Four Fs of positive parent-child negotiating:

• *Fairness.* Show fairness by keeping your conversation focused on the present, by forgetting the past, by focusing on laying the groundwork for the future, and, above all, by refraining from pointing the finger of blame at anyone.

• *Flexibility.* Show flexibility by being ready to listen to your child. Don't try to force a preconceived solution. Change what can be changed.

• *Friendliness.* Show friendliness by being warm and encouraging throughout the discussion.

• *Firmness.* Show firmness by making clear that you are determined to reach an agreement and to uphold your end of any bargain.

Now let's explore each of these Four Fs of positive negotiation in a little more depth.

Fairness. A dangerous diversion as you enter into the negotiation process is to bring up past transgressions. Some parents will say, "Okay, son, now we've got an agreement. But I just want to be sure that you're not going to let me down the way you did two months ago . . ."

People seem more eager to lodge blame than to reach a lasting solution that will improve the future of a relationship. Yet no one, including a child, is going to be happy or experience any benefit from having blame placed squarely on his head. Accusations, criticisms, or snide remarks will undercut the possibility of trusting relationships. Such finger-pointing can even sound the death knell for an otherwise effective negotiation. To keep the emotional temperature low, don't make accusations about past errors.

Never resort to sarcasm. Cutting comments are cheap shots when dealing with youngsters. The very young won't understand your sarcasm; they're likely to be bewildered by it, or by any comments they can't quite understand. Older youngsters, not knowing how to defend themselves against a sharp tongue, will probably become hostile or sullen. It is particularly important to watch for sarcasm; its presence could be a sign that your efforts to keep calm are not completely effective.

Flexibility. As your meeting proceeds, be ready to listen closely and objectively—with an open mind—to your youngster's side of the story. Let him go first, before you offer your own suggestions. If your youngster gets a bad introduction to negotiating, he may be alienated and refuse to participate at all. He will be quick to sense that you have a fixed idea of what the outcome of the meeting is going to be, sometimes even when you don't!

As you begin to test your skills as an honest negotiator, apply your powers of persuasion with utmost respect for the interests of the other side. Remember: A negotiation implies benefits to both parties—and they must be benefits both parties are able to see. Everyone has a lot to lose if negotiations break down. You may get your way temporarily, even if your child gets nothing. But the peace you achieve in your household will probably not last very long.

Friendliness. There are solid practical reasons for keeping the discussion light and easy. If you approach the negotiating meeting with a relaxed, open attitude, and can keep things moving along, whatever obstacles appear, you'll be much more likely to end up with an agreement you like. In addition your personal relationship with your child will improve. You know as well as I do that youngsters often say unexpected, delightful things, and an intense, one-on-one meeting like this can be an occasion for fun as well as family business. So be prepared for the unexpected. And if humor seems in order, always be sure to laugh *with* your children and not *at* them.

Firmness. Your child may have heard you threaten many times and have learned long ago when it's safe to ignore your threats. He may also be accustomed to broken promises. Most parents do want to keep the promises they make. And certainly, children are very careful to remind them if they forget. But sometimes a promise is broken because parents feel that the child has committed some breach of behavior that negates the original promise. They consequently withdraw their promise as a way of punishing the child.

When children learn to expect such conduct from their parents, promises lose much of their power to motivate the child's actions. In agreements hammered out in negotiations, however, it's extremely important that the promised benefits be given when the child has upheld his end of the bargain— no matter what else he may have done. And it's equally critical that you *not* deliver a promised benefit if the child has not carried out his obligations.

In other words, you must convey your sense of firmness in the way that you conclude your agreement, so that your child will know that a solemn contract has been made. Otherwise, the settlements you reach will be just a meaningless exercise.

If you can maintain these four critical attitudes—these Four Fs of positive negotiating—you should be able to *enjoy* the meeting with your child. The discussion should be fun as well as challenging for both of you.

Principle of Positive Persuasion 2.
Be clear about rules.

Although most families operate with some sort of rules for their children, these rules may not always be clear in everyone's mind. It's very important for each member of the family, including the children, to *understand* the fundamental family rules and policies. It's also quite helpful when both parents and children can participate in forming those rules. That way everyone has a stake in abiding by them. As a matter of fact, getting an agreement about just what a family's rules are can be one of the major tasks in getting any negotiation to succeed.

One of the first things you may learn when you consider negotiating over a problem is that you aren't sure exactly what household policies are being violated. Somehow your child's behavior annoys you, but it's hard to pinpoint just what the problem behavior is. Perhaps you think your child is too saucy, or he answers back, or he's noisy, or he's disobedient or quarrelsome or perhaps demanding. But such observations are far too general to be used in outlining the rules for a useful negotiation. If you can't say *exactly* what's wrong, you can be sure that your child—whose understanding is so much less than yours—will be unable to do any better.

I've often been present in a home where the parents decide to reprimand a child, even though exactly what the child has done is extremely vague. The children can't say what it is; the parents don't seem to be able to describe the transgression; and, for that matter, I can't put it into words either! Such a situation can lead to bad feelings and even chaos. There should never be any confusion as to what the rules are and what the violations are.

What seems at first to be a general rule violation, such as "talking back," has to be broken down into much more specific, recognizable actions. Children understand specific rules best. We develop an understanding of more general rules only as we grow older.

When you think back over the way you've been relating to your child, you may find to your surprise that you've been very inconsistent in applying your rules. Your applications may have depended as much on your mood or fleeting feelings toward the child as on the child's actual behavior. So it's imperative to decide first just what the rules are going to be. Then you'll have an objective standard to rely upon no matter how you may feel at a given moment.

In addition to settling upon definite family rules, you can also help to keep your negotiations clear and straightforward by keeping to the topic at hand. Inevitably all sorts of irrelevant topics will come up in a first conversation with your child. So always be ready to refocus your discussion on the central issue. If the problem involves your child's homework, stick to the homework. Don't let the conversation wander off into a consideration of your child's misuse of the family car.

In short, be ready to *state clearly* what the specific problem is, and then avoid being diverted.

Principle of Positive Persuasion 3.
Be willing to engage in some give-and-take.

In negotiating a settlement with your child, it's important to understand that the first offer you make may not be the one that's finally accepted. There often has to be a considerable amount of give-and-take before solutions are reached at a bargaining table. We all have our very special and individual "hot buttons" that need to be identified and pressed before we are motivated to change our behavior—and young children are certainly no exception.

Every time one mother went to the supermarket with her five-year-old daughter, she found herself annoyed and embarrassed because her little girl persisted in handling everything in sight. The youngster often picked items off the shelf and put them into the shopping cart—when the mother didn't want to buy them. Understandably the mother was concerned because her shopping was being disrupted. She also worried that the store detective might suspect she was shoplifting! Shopping had become a burdensome task, a tremendous strain for both mother and daughter. Usually an outing ended with the child crying and the mother angry.

Then the mother learned about the possibilities of negotiation. One day, before going out to the market, the adult suggested that if the youngster would refrain from touching things on the shelves, she would be entitled to a treat at the end of the shopping. Knowing her child's likes and dislikes, the mother made some suggestions as to the particular treat that the girl might want.

At first the daughter responded with a rather unreasonable counteroffer: she wanted some very expensive candy for her reward! But the mother made a further counteroffer—a cost limitation on the item the girl could earn. On the other hand, the youngster could choose the item *all by herself.* After a little discussion of the amount of the upper limit, the daughter finally agreed and immediately began to spend most of each shopping expedition discussing what treat she would pick. The fact that she would be given complete power over her choice was enough to offset the restriction on the cost.

During this decision-making process, the mother achieved some degree of peace. Just as important, the child learned how to reach a compromise and how to make some simple decisions for herself. All this was possible because the parent was willing to encourage a little give-and-take.

As another example, one father wanted his teenage son to mow the family lawn, and he wanted it done on Friday afternoon, in preparation for the weekend. As it happened, this desire was not realistic. The teenager was deeply involved in high school athletics, and on a typical Friday afternoon he devoted most of his time to practicing the sport of the season. Then, being a social fellow, he would rush home, bolt down a quick supper, and get ready for his Friday-night date.

Obviously he had more interesting things to do with his free time than mow the lawn. And that automatically put him and his father in conflict. The father was insisting that his son do something that was very "costly" for the boy. But because their mutual antagonism had grown so strong, the parent wasn't willing even to consider a compromise. He wanted to force his solution on his son. "It's a matter of principle," he told the boy. But his son wouldn't buy this explanation.

After a couple of unpleasant arguments, the father finally wised up: he saw that his own belligerence was making things worse. He decided to try some negotiation. He asked his son to meet with him quietly one Sunday afternoon, when neither had any other pressing engagements. The only item on the agenda was how to get the lawn mowed without interfering with the youngster's school and social schedule.

The son often wanted transportation on his weekend dates, but his father usually said that the family car was needed by the parents. So the father, rather than lecturing the boy about family responsibilities, simply made an offer: "I'd like you to mow the lawn once a week, and I'd like us to set a time that will be convenient to both of us. In return for this service that you'll provide, I'll let you use the family car once a week. What do you say?"

The son thought about the offer, and after a few remarks he got down to the real issue. "The problem is that you always want me to mow the lawn when I just can't seem to do it."

"Well," the father replied. "Maybe that's the key thing we need to resolve. When would be a *good* time for you to mow it?"

The boy reflected for a moment or two. "You want it ready for the weekend, right?"

"Right," the father replied.

"Okay, what about if I do it on Thursday afternoon after I get in from baseball practice? Or maybe early Saturday morning?"

The Thursday proposal sounded best to the father, and he quickly agreed. The two also settled on Friday night for the boy's dates, with the understanding that he could also use the car on Saturday nights at least three times a month. Each party understood that he would have to keep his end of the bargain. If the solution broke down, they would meet again to renegotiate the terms.

In this case, both the son and the father gained something significant from their brief negotiation. Both went away quite satisfied, and most important of all, a source of friction in the family disappeared.

Principle of Positive Persuasion 4.
Focus on one thing at a time.

In negotiating with children, it's wise to try to change only one aspect of your child's behavior at a time, not to effect a complete reformation. It's important to home in on simple and concrete goals. Stay away from broad personality deficiencies such as your youngster's lack of consideration or his irresponsibility.

One negotiation broke down because the mother introduced too many factors for either her or her son to deal with in one session. She said, "There are several things that you're not doing that are bothering me, and I want to see if we can do something to clear them all up this weekend. For one thing, you're not mowing the lawn regularly. For another, you almost never hang up your clothes. And you're not taking out the garbage, as you agreed to do. Now, what do you suggest that we do about these things?"

Because she was overly negative and a little strident, this woman opened the negotiation in a way that almost stopped the whole attempt in its tracks. But she had the wisdom to demonstrate flexibility and open-mindedness by giving her son the opportunity to suggest solutions to their problems. She at least got the discussion going.

But unfortunately she had introduced too many issues, and that made the discussion too complicated. She and her son kept hopping back and forth between the lawn, the clothes, and the garbage. Soon they both got confused over what kind of behavior would be acceptable to the mother in each situation and what sort of benefits would be attractive to the son.

The more experienced you get in negotiating, the easier it will become to deal with several topics at once. But in general—and especially when you're just learning how—I recommend that you focus on finding a negotiated solution for only one problem at a time.

Principle of Positive Persuasion 5.
Avoid subtle and not-so-subtle negative pressures.

As I've mentioned, no negatives should be introduced into any negotiating sessions. It's important to avoid threats of dire consequences if a child takes or fails to take certain action. This tactic should be easy to recognize and avoid.

Neither should there be any "or elses." So don't say, "This is my final offer—you take it *or else.*" If the child doesn't agree to an initial offer, avoid issuing threats to stop negotiating; instead, talk some more and especially listen some more.

Be careful to show your willingness to negotiate at all times. For example, avoid sighs that say, "I've tried and tried, but you just won't cooperate!" Remember that there are more ways than talk that express your discontent with your child.

Even if you're considering depriving your youngster of something, try to put the concept in a positive way. One mother, for instance, made the following overly negative offer while negotiating over an eating problem: "If you don't eat your dinner, you won't get any dessert!" From the perspective of effective, persuasive negotiations, there's a wide world of difference between this statement and saying, "If you finish your dinner, you'll please me greatly, and get your favorite dessert."

Among the many ways of staying positive, some may not immediately come to mind unless you've already done a considerable amount of negotiation. For example:

• When you say something positive, you use a different

tone of voice than when you speak negatively. Children, just like adults, will respond constructively or unhelpfully to the tone in your voice.

• By offering a reward instead of a punishment, you'll be giving your child something to strive for, something to achieve, not just something to avoid. You're saying, in effect, "I want to help you become a better person by learning family responsibility . . . by getting along with your siblings . . . or by completing your homework." As the child matures, he'll come to see for himself that these duties carry built-in rewards. But he'll never reach this point if he doesn't learn to carry out the duties in the first place.

The rewards you offer help to reinforce good qualities you hope to develop in your child. Threats, punishments, or negative statements, in contrast, tend to cause the child to associate these very same qualities with bad consequences.

• You can reduce the possibility of rebellion in your child by emphasizing the positive. Many parents who dwell on what's going to happen to the child if he doesn't do what they want will get the belligerent answer, "I don't care!" These words signal hostility and rebellion. And with such a beginning, feelings and emotions can escalate into family war. Even the calmest of adults may begin to lose control when confronted with an "I don't care!" retort. So keep your conversation upbeat and nonthreatening and you won't antagonize your child.

For these reasons, avoiding negative pressures is very advantageous in negotiating. But often when I suggest that parents give their children things in return for an agreement to perform certain actions or services, I hear: "But that's a bribe!"

This objection frequently comes up when the discussion involves certain changes in behavior—such as doing homework—which are perceived as more for the child's ultimate benefit than the parents'. And it's true, of course, that many tasks parents set for their children *are* for the child's ultimate benefit. Learning to read may not be fun, but it's extremely beneficial in the long run. Parents often feel that their child should understand this fact—and that the long-term rewards should be enough.

Unfortunately, however, children, being children, aren't always able to act sensibly (at least in grown-up terms); they just can't see the long-term benefits that their parents may tell them will come at some future time. Instead, given their limited experience, they act more in the here and now. Whatever their parents may say, they know that right now, reading or violin lessons or whatever discipline their parents want them to learn is difficult; and there are much more enjoyable things they could be doing. Eventually they'll learn to work for more distant rewards; but until they do, parents will have limited success if they try to force their own understanding on their child.

So your child should *see* clearly the advantages in the agreements you make. Perhaps if you explain the long-term advantages of an act, the child will accept the explanation and be willing to agree that a long-term benefit is an adequate reward for his actions. But it's more likely that he won't be able to see as far ahead as you can. So be alert: what's persuasive for you, especially as far as distant rewards are concerned, won't necessarily persuade your child. And if your child doesn't see a gain, there has not been a satisfactory negotiation.

You'll probably find you often have to rely on short-term rewards for younger children. But don't fall into the trap of equating these rewards with bribes. A bribe, by definition, is a payment made "under the table," illegally or immorally, to influence a person to act in an illegal or immoral way. If you're dealing in an aboveboard fashion in your negotiations with your child, arranging for him to carry out beneficial and desirable actions, you're not involved in bribery!

In any case, your persuasiveness should be rooted in honesty and credibility. If you insist that the child accept your concept of what should be rewarding, you'll tend to be devious rather than straightforward, or you'll try to browbeat your child into an agreement that should be unforced.

One reason that the benefits offered in negotiations may appear to be bribery lies in the types of rewards that parents often find most meaningful to young children. For example, privileges and favorite foods are a typical benefit that many children readily accept. And if parents have assumed that beneficial acts should be done only "for their own sake," such treats can certainly appear to be payoffs.

Parents are right to feel that treats shouldn't be handed out in an impersonal or begrudging manner. The attention and approval that go along with rewards are extremely important. In fact, parental attention and affectionate interactions with children are *in themselves* very rewarding for youngsters who live in happy homes. Often an appropriately timed display of parental approval for the child's behavior will be reward enough.

A key element in any loving relationship is the satisfaction the giver gains from the pleasure experienced by the beloved receiver. This satisfaction is known to every loving mother and father. A child's smile can be a big reward for hours of arduous care. Mothers so rewarded can never say they get nothing from their children for all the care they receive! Similarly a mother's smile and affectionate touches can reward cooperation from a loving child. This mutual satisfaction in pleasing a beloved person is a key element in the success of *all* the negotiating strategies in this book.

One mother I know was having trouble getting her young son to eat his supper each evening. Like many other six-year-olds, he would play with his food, get distracted, and often leave more than half of each helping on his plate. She tried nagging, but that didn't work. So she decided to take a different tack. She explained once again how important it was for him to finish his meal—but this time, she did it in a friendly way, just before mealtime. Then she *ignored* any dawdling he did over his food; but when he did eat two or three spoonfuls, she immediately praised him, smiled, and gave him a quick hug.

Almost miraculously, this method had an immediate payoff. The boy was so pleased at the sudden shift in his mother's attention that he began to eat more and more quickly, until before long he had reached a normal pace. The mother also made a great fuss about how pleased she was when he finally finished his meal. As a result, his willingness to eat nutritious foods improved considerably.

This arrangement completely eliminated nagging or threats of punishment. The boy's obvious pleasure pleased the mother at least as much as his better eating habits did, and everyone left the table happier and more satisfied.

Principle of Positive Persuasion 6.
Be ready to experiment.

Let's suppose you do everything right:

- You keep all your remarks positive.
- You create a warm and pleasant atmosphere for your first negotiating session.

- You offer several compromise solutions to the problem under consideration.
- You are ready to listen carefully.

But nothing works. You simply can't reach an agreement. Or if you have settled on something, you find yourself quickly back at the negotiating table with the deal in shambles.

Many parents have these problems in their first negotiations. Your child probably doesn't know how to act in the strange situation, and you may be just feeling your own way along. Don't feel you're alone or you're doomed to failure. Instead, it's important to see negotiation with your child as a time to experiment.

Here you as a parent have a great advantage over professional negotiators in business or government. You know your "opposite number"—your child—better than any regular negotiator knows the other party. So if nothing seems to be working, sit back for a moment and consider what really makes your child tick.

When a negotiation can't be concluded satisfactorily, or when it doesn't last, you should first consider the compensation your child is receiving. The arrangement by which he is to be paid may be too complicated; the rewards may be too remote; or you may not be able to find anything your child wants that isn't already his for free.

As a general rule, it's best to experiment with immediate rewards for very young children. In most cases, rewards that will become available only several days or perhaps even hours into the future won't be meaningful to a child younger than seven or eight. Rewards must be seen as rewards by the child. Even those that carry real advantages may not be effective in influencing his behavior if they are too far away.

So suppose you promise: "If you eat all your dinner every

night this week, I'll feel so good about it that I'll take you to the zoo on Saturday." In such a case, the promise may very well fail to make an impression. It might be better to offer an inexpensive toy that you can place immediately in your child's hands, or some favorite food.

I know one father who came up with the idea of buying an inexpensive bag of plastic cowboy figures as rewards to induce better eating habits. Every evening just before supper, he would pull out one of the figures and put it up on a shelf next to the dinner table. "That will be yours if you eat a good meal tonight," he would tell his four-year-old son. Invariably the boy would pack away the food, even as he cut his eyes around at that figure up on the shelf.

Of course you know your own child better than anyone else does. And some young children may, against all expectations, respond quite well to a delayed reward. I'm reminded of another four-year-old, a young girl who had her heart set on a dress for her favorite doll. She was willing to concentrate hard on dressing herself for an entire week, all the time being motivated by the promise that she would get that piece of doll's apparel the following weekend.

On the other hand, even an older child may need an instant reward, especially at first, if he's distrustful, or just getting used to the process of negotiation. Sometimes a preteen or teenager needs to be assured with some concrete, immediate benefit that this strange new bargaining system is really going to work.

One eleven-year-old entered quite readily into a negotiation that was designed to get him to clean up his room regularly. But he preferred the immediate—and inexpensive—reward of getting some homemade popcorn along with a few minutes to chat with his mother just after the room was cleaned. In fact he chose this benefit over the possibility of a longer-term but more costly benefit like going to see a popular movie the next weekend. After this youngster came to trust the negotiating process, he was more willing to accept delayed, future benefits. Why? He had greater confidence that those benefits would actually be forthcoming.

If you remain flexible and are willing to experiment with every aspect of your reward system, you'll eventually succeed. Don't worry if you don't reach an agreement at your first negotiating session. Just plan another meeting, and ask your child to come prepared with some new ideas about what *he* wants from the negotiating process. Before the next meeting occurs, try to ascertain more clearly what your child's interests and aspirations are. That way, you'll be in a better position to conclude a meaningful commitment.

A major reason experimentation is so important is that adults can't so easily see that what seems to be a worthy reward to them may not be at all what sparks the imagination of a child. One mother who had enrolled her son in Suzuki violin lessons found this out in no uncertain terms. The three-year-old enjoyed the formal lessons well enough, but he hated the daily practice. Fine motor coordination was just developing in his fingers, and it was difficult for him to press the right strings with any facility. In short, he wasn't making the music he liked to hear.

The mother, though, was persistent. She first tried cajoling and pleading with him, but that didn't work. He had learned she would eventually give up trying. Then she shifted to a reward system. They agreed he would get an extra hour of TV time for every day the practice was done. But the child simply didn't respond positively.

Soon it appeared that the agreement was not going to work. Arguments continued, and the boy seldom earned the TV time. Finally, when virtually at the end of her rope, she hit upon the answer as she observed her son wandering through a variety store. He was particularly drawn to bright-colored stickers, and especially stick-on stars. So she bought a bunch of the stars and other stickers, pulled out a spiral notebook, and put together her offer: She offered the youngster one star every period that he practiced for ten minutes, and he would be allowed to place his stars in the special spiral notebook. The idea enthralled the three-year-old, and this reward system worked for weeks. It was immediate and was accompanied by the mother's pleased and affectionate attention. Finally the boy became more skillful in playing his violin, and soon he didn't need this reward system anymore.

As you apply these Principles of Positive Persuasion in negotiating with your child, remember that you're not merely applying abstract techniques of manipulation. Instead you're trying to understand your youngster's underlying motivations. Your goal is to harness those motivations to help your child grow into the adult you would like him to be.

In emphasizing the positive and trying different approaches to negotiation, you'll develop an extra sensitivity to your child's special interests and orientations. As you do, you'll begin to realize that the bedrock foundation of any persuasive parental style is learning to understand your child almost as well as you understand yourself.

In any negotiation, an awareness of your child's needs and a desire to help him realize his greatest potential is critical. With such an attitude, the specific techniques that comprise the nuts and bolts of negotiation will flow naturally and freely from your normal, loving family relationships.

3.

The Nuts and Bolts of Give-and-Take

*A*NY good relationship between parents and children has to be rooted deeply in love. Most responsible, loving parents know that. So they'll say:

- "I want my child to have the very best."
- "I love my child more than life itself."
- "I'm willing to postpone spending money on myself if I can just provide my youngster with a good education . . . a great athletic experience . . . or any chance to succeed in a big way in life."

Still, what does all this mean in practice? We *say* we love our children. But in the frenetic, fast-moving, jam-packed stream of daily life, how do we express that love?

Unfortunately, many parents sometimes get in such a rush meeting the demands of their daily schedules that they leave little time to help their children with important youthful problems. A parent may know what his son should do. So he tells him—in fact, *commands* him—to do it in no uncertain terms. He expects his sons and daughters to see solutions to problems as quickly and thoroughly as he does, and to respond without questioning when they're told to do something. And he talks to his children in terms he would never dream of using with his friends or business associates.

Most parents believe that they know best. Understandably they become disturbed when they see negative patterns becoming ingrained in their child's behavior—like a tendency to be argumentative or to sulk.

Unfortunately, however, getting an important point across to an independent teenager—or preschooler for that matter —requires more than military mannerisms. The ultimate motive behind those barking commands may well be a loving concern about your youngster's future. But to be accepted, those important points must be communicated in love as well. And that's really what negotiating with children is all about.

Negotiation is a practical means of expressing parental love to children and clearing the path for children to express their love toward parents. So far, we've laid a broad foundation for negotiation by discussing the principles of a persuasive parental style. Because these principles are practical in a variety of situations, we'll continue to keep them in mind and apply them as we take up the nitty-gritty of a negotiating session.

But much more needs to be said on this practical level if your efforts at negotiation are to succeed. Consequently we want to focus now in more detail on some of the specific negotiating tactics that comprise the "nuts and bolts of give-and-take."

Tactic 1. Pay attention to your timing.

Since the late 1960s and all through the 1970s, we've heard people tell us, "Get in touch with your feelings!" This advice from the realm of pop psychology has become so commonplace that it's past the point of banality. Many have relegated it to the category of psychobabble—the collection of vague words and phrases culled from popularized psychology and used so often that they have been rendered meaningless.

As you've probably surmised by now, I'm a psychologist who prefers to concentrate on actual events in a person's experience. I prefer to focus concretely on what people think, feel, and do. I'm not so interested in nebulous notions such as understanding yourself or plumbing the depths of your personality.

At the same time, when it comes to effective negotiation, I don't want to downgrade the importance of what people feel. Feelings are of critical importance in any negotiation: they can help, or they can cripple the entire process. But I think we can best talk about feelings in the context of what is being done, said, or thought—not as phenomena divorced from what's happening around us.

It's especially important to try to understand *before* a negotiation begins exactly what feelings are likely to be operative. You should have a sense of how feelings will impede or facilitate the movement toward a meaningful settlement. For example, as we've already seen, if you or your youngster is angry about the issue to be discussed, that's not the time to begin a negotiation. And it's a warning that anger may quickly surface when the topic arises again. On the other hand, if one or both of you are feeling the pinch from a particular problem, the timing may be just right. In other words, sometimes you have to let a situation simmer for a while.

I'm reminded of one father who got quite excited about the idea of negotiating—but then tried to push the concept on his twelve-year-old daughter. The main problem was that the issue he wanted to negotiate was too touchy at the time he tried to force a discussion. During dessert one evening, the father said, "Mary, I've come across this great idea in talking to a psychologist I know. I think it could do wonders for some of the arguments that you and I have. You know— we're always disagreeing about whether you can go to over-night parties at a friend's house. I know you've been wanting to go to Jenny Smith's place this weekend. So I'd like to spend some time talking about this problem right after dinner."

As it happened, the girl had just had an argument with her mother about that weekend's plans a few hours before, and the issue was still very sensitive for her. So she claimed she was involved in an extracurricular school art project that had to be finished that evening. She responded, "Aw, Dad, I've got some other stuff I've got to do tonight. Can't we talk about this later?"

The father, not getting the signals that his timing was off, continued to push the topic. He in effect *required* his daugh-ter to sit down with him for a few minutes after dinner. She, as might be expected, resisted him at every point during the discussion—and yet another argument ensued. In fact, the altercation came on so suddenly that she never got a chance to learn how accommodating her father might have been. His attempt to negotiate a settlement never even got off the ground.

The concept of negotiation is going to be strange to many children, just as it is to many parents. And some gentle educa-tion and effective persuasion may be necessary just to get a child to sit down and begin to engage in a little give-and-take.

Children may fear that the "price" at the end of the agree-ment will be too high, and they'll resort to the familiar tactics of obstruction or stubbornness. Also, parental discussions may have too many negative overtones for the child to see any advantages in such an approach. It may even be off-putting to mention the word *negotiation.* Timing is frequently an all-important consideration for success.

One ten-year-old boy named Johnny was not only not ready to negotiate a problem he was facing, he was actually primed not to negotiate. Johnny's difficulty was that even though he was moving rapidly toward adolescence, he still refused to eat many foods, just as he had refused as an infant. He lived on a very restricted diet, limited almost exclusively to hot dogs with ketchup, potato chips, and ice cream.

His mother wasn't too happy about his nutritional habits, and the home atmosphere was continually clouded with arguments and hard feelings about food. From time to time, Johnny's mother tried a variety of tactics in an attempt to get him to eat—even including an effort at negotiations: She offered his favorite foods if he would agree to eat other, more nourishing fare. But Johnny always refused these offers. After the mother's attempts at persuasion and argument failed, she invariably would give in to Johnny's demands.

In most other ways, Johnny was a sweet and agreeable child, though he could be very stubborn when he didn't get his own way. His parents were friendly, agreeable people, and on the whole I discovered the family relationships to be quite affectionate.

As the parents and I began to discuss Johnny's problem further, some special facts emerged that helped to explain why he was so stubborn about foods. Since infancy, when he first showed his strong food opinions, his mother had complied with his demands for his favorite eats without much opposition. If Johnny refused one food, she would offer another. Of course such an approach can be quite natural and even praiseworthy—so long as good nutrition is maintained.

But unfortunately, instead of developing a wide range of food preferences during this process of sampling various foods, Johnny narrowed his mealtime selections. Worse, he learned that if he refused a particular food, another would almost always be offered. All he had to do was go through the foods that his mother suggested until he finally found one that was his favorite. It wasn't that he detested all the foods that were offered to him; he just knew that if he held out long enough, he would be offered one that was the sweetest and tastiest of all.

After we discussed the problem, Mom decided to try negotiating again. She tried offering Johnny's preferred foods on the condition that he would also try some others at the same time. Her first attempt got off to a poor start. Johnny refused every offer. After all, he had learned through years of past experience that all he had to do was hold out!

Then the mother switched to another tactic. She offered other services and privileges if he would only eat nutritious foods, but Johnny refused everything, even offers that seemed far too expensive or fantastic to the mother. Again, Johnny was operating from his past experience: He had learned that Mom would always take his refusals as a cue to offer something even better, and that was exactly what was happening.

The essence of the problem was that Johnny didn't know the first thing about how to negotiate, and so all the mother's efforts failed miserably. The timing may never be right for the most difficult negotiating problems unless you first pave the way with easier issues. So we decided to try to get Johnny used to negotiating procedures by focusing on some simpler problems, where agreement would come more quickly. That way Johnny would get the hang of the procedure and we might be able to return to the more difficult food problems later. This approach, by the way, can be an excellent tactic for families who are not experienced negotiators. It's especially helpful if feelings about some particular problem—such as Johnny's food difficulties—run quite high.

As it happened, Johnny was inconsistent about putting away his coat, books, and other things he brought into the house. Typically they would litter the floor for hours, even after he had received several reminders from his mother. She usually ended up putting the things away herself.

The family had never regarded this as a serious problem, and emotions never grew too intense over the subject. So we decided to focus on this particular problem first. Mom noted that Johnny wanted a baseball glove and, unbeknownst to Johnny, the parents had already decided to give him one. But she and her husband thought that it would be a good motivator to tie the giving of the baseball glove to the pickup of the coat, books, and other items. So Mom offered Johnny a deal. She would keep track of the times Johnny put away his things when he came in from outside. When he got to eighty times without being told or reminded, he would earn his glove. In presenting this proposal, however, the mother made it clear that Johnny could have some input about the number of times it would take to earn the glove. He immediately began to offer excuses about why eighty times was too much, and finally the two of them agreed that fifty pickups would be appropriate. Mom was also to keep a record of Johnny's pickups on a sheet on the side of the refrigerator, where he could clearly see how he was doing. The glove was a distant reward, so we were taking a chance. But the negotiation went quite smoothly, and so did another one that they arranged on another issue the next week.

Now we felt that Johnny was ready for the "biggie" once more—the all-important eating issue. This time Johnny showed more interest as a negotiator when the subject of his food habits was presented to him. Mom also detected more understanding and generosity on his part. When she took him aside and began to explain to him how worried she was about his diet, he listened closely. He was attentive as she explained that she had tried to negotiate before, but she had dropped the attempt because their discussions just hadn't worked out. "But now," she said, "I think we're ready to discuss your eating seriously."

Throughout this discussion, the mother controlled herself very well. She made no comments about how tired she was of being a "short-order cook for one person," as she had often said in the past. No accusations, no finger-pointing. Before long, they had reached an agreement on the difficult food problem. Johnny agreed to eat two ounces of the food Mom prepared for the rest of the family at each meal. Then he would get his regular, favorite fare. They also agreed that when he had eaten this small portion without any complaints for twenty meals, he would be able to join his dad to see a baseball game. And they agreed that if things went well, they would renegotiate after two weeks to increase the portions of the regular food.

Not only did Johnny and his mother reach a settlement as a result of these negotiations, they also found that the agreement worked smoothly in practice. It seemed like a miracle to Mom, but soon Johnny had completely abandoned his limited diet. In my opinion, the major problem we had overcome was Johnny's persistent refusal to consider alternatives to his eating habits. He had been simply unaware of the benefits of expanding his diet. Stubbornness and refusal had been his methods of "negotiating" until we showed him another way.

In short, we lost out at first in our negotiating because the food problem was too difficult to tackle first, and the time to deal with it would never be right until he had learned some negotiating skills with simpler problems. It's just like learning arithmetic—first the simple problems, then the harder ones. It was essential for Johnny to learn something about negotiating procedures by dealing with easier problems first.

Tactic 2. Recognize that each party to a negotiation must gain something.

It's possible to achieve the goals of discipline through a negotiated settlement—*if* you can forget the idea of depriving and begin to think in terms of *giving* as well as *gaining.* You provide some benefit in place of anything that may have to be taken away.

One family confronted a difficult situation on three separate occasions over a period of several weeks. But they responded in quite a different way each time. The ten-year-old son wanted to see a program on television rather than going to bed at his regular time. The parents, on the other hand, had a favorite program that they wanted to see. The parents had two choices. They could either permit their boy to stay up late and watch his show—and miss their own—or they could insist that he go directly to bed.

The first time these parents faced this problem, they made the first choice. They let their youngster have his way. The boy was quite happy but the parents weren't—mainly because the television interfered with their evening. Not only were they unable to watch the program they wanted to see, the boy insisted on keeping the television turned up to a relatively loud and distracting level. The noise disturbed them even when they retired to an adjoining room. To make matters worse, the youngster did everything possible to keep from turning the volume down. He might actually soften the sound for a while, but then when they turned their backs, he would creep over and edge it up to the level that he preferred. Gradually the anger in both father and mother began to build. Finally the father burst out, "Turn that thing down!" The mother, for her part, became more silent and withdrawn as the evening progressed. After the father's outburst, the ten-year-old went to seek comfort from his mother, but he found her very unreceptive. A generally uncomfortable atmosphere had developed because the parents had gained nothing of value—in fact, had lost a great deal—as a result of this uneasy settlement.

A couple of weeks later, a similar situation arose. The youngster wanted to see a special cartoon feature on TV that would run past his regular bedtime. This time the sequence of events was different, but equally unsatisfactory. When the boy made his request to see the program, the father, remembering the last incident, shouted, "No! You certainly can't stay up late to watch television. You remember what happened last time!" And he angrily sent the youngster to bed, in effect punishing him for even asking for a benefit. The boy was quite hurt and ran off to his room crying. On this occasion he received some comfort from his mother, but the event left resentment against his father and a feeling that he had been treated unfairly. This state of affairs didn't make it any easier for the parents to enjoy their night together. The father, feeling guilty, fell into a bad mood; the mother pondered most of the evening why it was so hard to achieve peace in their household.

In this situation, the parents really loved their child, and the child loved his parents. But, through ignorance about how to deal with one difficult situation, they found themselves in a no-win situation, an emotional box canyon with no peaceful exit.

Then the mother discovered negotiation. She and her husband discussed ways that they might be able to express their love for their child through an informal bargaining system. Finally they resolved to move ahead with this approach when the timing seemed right.

Sure enough, within a few days their ten-year-old made a tentative, self-conscious overture to his mother (whom he suspected would be more receptive) about the possibility of viewing a late television special that had been recommended by a teacher at his school.

"It sounds interesting to me, but why don't you ask your father about it?" the mother replied.

"You know that won't do any good!" the boy said. "He'll probably send me to bed again."

"I don't think he will this time—but why don't we both try it?" the mother said.

Clearly the time was ripe for negotiation. In fact the boy would probably have been willing to try almost anything to regain the right to stay up to see an occasional television program. The parents were also primed because they wanted to eliminate the tension that had resulted from the television issue in their home.

So the boy approached his father, and the father immediately agreed to discuss the subject. "I can understand that you want to watch television, but we've had some problems with this matter in the past," the father began. "Maybe the problem has been partly with me. But let's see if we can work it out, okay?"

"Okay," the boy replied. He was amazed. His father had admitted he might have been wrong!

"Now you tell me exactly what you want, and then we'll try to work something out," the father continued.

At this point, the youngster explained simply that he wanted to watch this program—and he bolstered his argument by saying that the suggestion for viewing it had come originally from his teacher. The father was quite receptive. But he laid down some clear ground rules that he felt would help balance the child's benefit with the parents' benefit.

For one thing, the father said that it was important to both parents that the volume of the television be kept quite low. Otherwise, they couldn't carry on a meaningful conversation. The father also suggested that in return for the privilege of watching this additional television, the boy should help clear the dinner table—a responsibility he had been neglecting recently. When the son had been doing this chore, he had tended to complain. Part of the deal was that he would have to do his job with no grumbling. These relatively easy restrictions were a mild pill for the boy to swallow in return for the upcoming television benefit.

In short, negotiation had transformed a no-win situation, where all parties were unhappy, into a win-win situation, where everybody stood to gain. Most important of all, this approach helped restore a peaceful, loving atmosphere in the family. For this compromise, the parents were happy to give up some of their television-watching time.

Tactic 3. Use "love signs" to express your love.

In parent-child negotiations, it's often enough of a benefit for a child just to feel that he has pleased his parents. I've known many children who have changed their behavior patterns simply because they wanted to make their parents happy. That happiness is the child's reward. But for this particular benefit to work, it's extremely important for parents to *show* how pleased they are when their child behaves in a commendable way.

One very bright little girl was having difficulty concentrat-

ing on her mathematics assignments in school. All the apti-
tude tests that she had taken indicated that she could easily
become a B or even an A student; but she kept coming up
with C's. The parents watched but said nothing as the girl's
performance slipped. Finally they became concerned
enough to approach the school. After conferences with her
teachers, the parents identified a major source of the problem: The girl was not making good use of her available study
time at school. She had an extremely busy round of extracurricular activities, including music lessons on two instruments.
There just didn't seem to be time for her to do any more
work at home unless she gave up some of these projects that
were so important to her. On the other hand, there *was* time
for her to get the work done at school if she just scheduled
herself better. But how to go about this?

The parents were stumped until they realized that they
were making a very easy-to-solve problem difficult. Their
daughter was quite parent-oriented. Being an only child, she
had gotten her major values from the role models that her
parents had provided for her; more than anything else, she
wanted to please them whenever she could.

As it turned out, all the mother and father had to do was
to ask the girl to sit down with them in a special family
conference and discuss the problem. As the child explained
it, she really hadn't even known that there *was* a problem!
Granted, her teacher kept encouraging her to work harder
and do better. But the girl thought that was just the way
teachers were supposed to act toward their students. She
didn't realize that she was being singled out because of some
particular problem in her work. "I'm not failing!" she told
her parents. "I'm really doing a lot better than many of the
other kids. I thought I was doing okay."

Her parents wisely took her at her word. Their discussion

now gave them an opportunity to explain in some detail that her aptitudes in math caused them and her teacher to expect more of her. She was very attentive and concerned—again, because she wanted very much to please. All the parents needed to do was to teach her how.

In a low-key way, without criticism that might produce feelings of pressure or guilt, they described what they felt she should be able to achieve. Then they suggested a program for her to reach the goal of better marks in her math classes. This involved finding specific times at school when she agreed she could devote her efforts to her math. They also proposed that she keep a record of how much studying she did.

The girl agreed to apply herself more strenuously to math during study periods at school. In addition, she chose a time when a friend was available who could give her help with troublesome concepts. And the parents responded positively, on a regular basis, to their child's progress so that she could see how much she was pleasing them.

The result? When her next grades came out, her teacher reported dramatic improvement—she was almost an A student.

Of course it's often necessary to provide more incentive than mere smiles or statements of pleasure from the parents. To this end, I suggest that parents consider upping the ante with what I call "love signs." These are special treats that a mother or father can give a youngster to reinforce statements that they are pleased with the child's behavior.

Love signs are not necessarily tied to a negotiation as an exchange item. Rather they are evidence of approval that should accompany quite naturally a parent's expressions of pleasure and love at the way a child is behaving.

Spontaneous hugs and kisses are common love signs. They

are a direct and physical way of saying "Thank you" or "You really did a good job, and I'm proud of you."

In some cases, however, love signs can be more tangible. One child got into the habit of complaining a great deal about having to go to bed. One evening his mother interrupted and explained to him that he was making her very unhappy, and that expression of her feelings was enough, in itself, to make him agree to stop his grousing.

Mother realized she needed to strengthen this agreement. She went on, telling him she loved him so much and appreciated his consideration of her so much that she would bake some of his favorite muffins for breakfast the next morning. Fortunately the child was as good as his word, and in the morning the mother's displays of appreciation, as well as her tasty muffins, confirmed that both parent and child were on a new route that promised more peaceful bedtimes.

As you can see, the mother didn't simply say, "If you'll go to bed without complaining, I'll bake you some muffins tomorrow morning." If she had taken that tack, the muffins would have been only a simple reward. Instead, she made it clear that the muffins were a sign of her affection. Perhaps the pleasure that he saw himself giving her would have been enough to stop the complaining before bedtime. But it never hurts to add an additional reinforcement, both to encourage the child to follow good behavior and to enhance the parent's pleasure.

It's natural and unavoidable for pleased parents to be more willing to please their child. By showing their pleasure clearly, they help pave the way for easier negotiations in the future. In short, this mother was quite wise in bolstering her child's commitment with a tasty treat.

I realize that love signs are common practice in many families. But we don't always take positive or negative actions toward each other with full knowledge of the impact of those actions, and love signs come almost as frequently whether a child has behaved well or badly. But if they are not offered purposefully, they don't serve as useful signals to the child.

It's probably much *more* natural for mothers to bake muffins for their children when the youngsters have been particularly pleasing and loving. Still these mothers may not tie such special treats to behavior. Often the child may see no relation between his actions and his parent's gesture. In any case, when parents want their child to cooperate and also want to use their own approval as a reward, it's helpful to have a personal history of backing up verbal approval with a more tangible reward.

It's important to ask yourself what your behavior is telling your child about the way people operate in the real world. A sensitive, intelligent use of love tokens in the negotiating process can prepare your child for the way he will often be treated in later years. For instance, when your boy becomes an adult and he graciously accedes to the legitimate wishes of someone else, what can he expect? Of course, the response from the other person will sometimes be ungracious. There may be a "thank you," but no reciprocal benefit. People who operate this way tend to be labeled as hypocrites. They seem grateful, but gratitude never emerges in concrete behavior. In most cases though, we anticipate that the recipient of a favor will not only be more friendly, but will also be inclined to bestow reciprocal benefits in the future.

Tactic 4. Formulate a "menu" of services or items you are willing to give your child.

The process of give-and-take presupposes that you have something to give that the child would like to take. It's axiomatic in parent-child negotiations that abstract benefits such as "good health" don't often have much influence and the rewards you offer may have to be more tangible. It's important to consult your options ahead of time and prepare a set of choices, called a "menu," to be used during negotiations.

Suppose that you want your child to begin to get to bed earlier. It will probably have no effect simply to say, "Early to bed, early to rise, makes a man healthy, wealthy, and wise." As Ben Franklin himself noted, it's unusual for people to act on wise advice! Parents more often get cooperation with their wise guidelines if they back them up with consequences: with rewards, or perhaps, regrettably, with punishments when their advice isn't heeded.

The first thing to do in formulating a menu of choices for your child is to consider the activities, toys, or other items that are important to him. There may be two or three dessert treats that he likes. Or perhaps she's collecting a certain set of dolls and dolls' clothing. Or maybe he's in the process of assembling a set of British soldiers or G.I. Joe figures.

As far as services are concerned, perhaps she's an ice-skating enthusiast and the Ice Capades are coming to town in a month. Or it could be that the circus or the local baseball team are his thing.

Whatever your child's particular interests, list them as your first step in formulating your menu. When you've completed the list, go over it and see what items you're sure you can deliver. Some things your child likes may simply be too expensive or too inaccessible to offer as realistic rewards in a negotiating session. On the other hand, if you don't list everything you can think of, you're likely to leave out some items that might be just the thing to use in your give-and-take.

You may want to eliminate some of those items that promise benefits too far in the future. With a very young child, it's important not to offer anything that is further away than today or tomorrow. You'll have more latitude in the rewards that you can offer to older youngsters who have a better concept of time *and* an intense desire to go to the circus or ice show relatively far off in the future.

Putting together a proper menu of rewards is an ongoing task. You can probably do an excellent, effective job just by sitting down for fifteen or twenty minutes and drawing up your initial list. But inevitably, as you begin to get into the process of negotiating, the benefits you plan to offer will have to be fine-tuned. Your child will have his say. Later on, as your experience with the items on the menu increases—and the child's experience grows—the menu will have to change. Items may be added or deleted, and the activities the child must do to earn them may be revised.

In any case, with menu in hand, you'll be ready to negotiate by making such offers as "If you are in bed by nine P.M., I'll come in and read you a story." Or "If you'll practice your violin twenty minutes in the afternoon, for three days, I'll let you invite a friend over for dinner."

It is important to include the child's input before any menu is finished. You may offer to allow your child to have one friend over for dinner if he plays the violin for five days. He, in turn, may be perfectly willing to play that violin for four days—in return for *two* friends. That may not be quite what you expected; but at least you're on the right track. You're working out a compromise and reaching a peaceful settlement.

Sometimes, of course, a parent will draw up a menu and then run into an immediate roadblock. At the beginning of that first negotiating session, the child will turn up her nose and say, "I don't want any of those things!" What do you do in this case? First, you remember that your menu was only intended as an initial step in the negotiation. It's just a means to help you start thinking. To help you know whether you've missed the mark in drawing up that list of rewards, the best thing to do is to direct the ball into your child's court. In other words, always ask *her* what she would like in the way of a reward. In effect you will be asking her to enter into the process of drawing up a menu. Second, you will want to consider whether your child is really saying that your prices are too high.

In some ways this approach puts you in the strongest possible position. Many effective business negotiators say that they prefer to ask the other party in a bargaining session to make the first offer. One businessman I know says, "If I'm trying to set up some sort of a joint venture, I never suggest exactly how the deal should be arranged—at least not at the outset. Instead, I let the other guy go first. And I'm usually pleasantly surprised. I find that I'm almost always willing to give more than he is content to accept."

Allowing your child to make the first offer in a negotiation often works quite well. If you allow him to name his reward, you may be pleasantly surprised at how modest his requests will be. Not only that, when a child is allowed to name his benefit, he's much more likely to be satisfied with it than if you name it.

Tactic 5. Remember your child's age.

I always cringe when I hear an adult begin to talk baby talk to youngsters. Of course simple language should be used to be sure your child understands all the terms. But I don't feel there is justification for using baby talk with a youngster of any age.

Those children who seem to be the most articulate and have the widest vocabularies are those with parents who have addressed them in mature language from toddlerhood. Your own child may begin to correct you if you talk to him in affected, nursery-room language. Children pick up the condescension.

Remember: In a negotiating session—as well as in any other communications with your children—you want them to know you expect reasonable responses from them. But if you treat them as babies, doing everything for them and making all their decisions, they're likely to *act* as babies.

As we've already seen, it's important for many young children to receive immediate rewards. If you tell a four- or five-year-old she will get something a month from now, she's very unlikely to respond as you'd wish. On the other hand, future rewards, so long as they're quite attractive, may work just fine with a ten- or eleven-year-old. But even then, when future rewards are promised, it's critical to provide frequent tangible evidence of progress toward those rewards—a point we'll discuss in detail in a later chapter.

In any case, you'll have to allow for more flexibility in negotiations as your child gets older. Some very young children are intelligent and savvy enough to know that they can make counteroffers and use other ploys to get more out of their parents than the adults originally planned to give. They should learn to do this better as they become more experienced in negotiating. When your child finally reaches the teen years, you'll discover that negotiations can become as complex as discussions over a labor-union contract. It's extremely important for parents to be ready to change their positions as their children become more adept at the process of give-and-take.

Don't become frustrated when your child begins to make

things a little tough for you and applies some pressure during the negotiations. After all, one of your objectives in launching negotiations has been to help your child develop his reasoning and language skills! You should be thankful that he's making you stretch, as the two of you work your way toward a settlement. Negotiating is not just a subtle way of getting what you have previously decided is best for your child; rather it's a process of mutually discovery.

Take the case of Ann, a fifteen-year-old who was deeply involved in ballet lessons after school. Ann and her mother first got into the negotiating process when the girl was about eleven. They made an arrangement that for four years went simply and smoothly. Ann was to call whenever her lesson would run past a given hour. A major problem cropped up, however, when Ann was about fifteen. She started coming home later than normal from her ballet lessons. She was breaking the long-standing rule that she should call whenever she was going to be late. When they finally spoke about the problem, the mother's feelings were already running high. The mother said, "You promised me you'd call when you were going to be late. But you don't call. You *know* how worried I get when you're not home on time."

"I only promised to call if I was able to!" Ann answered defensively. "I can't stop my lesson right in the middle and run to a phone, can I? Besides, the other girls never have to call their mothers."

But Ann's mother couldn't accept what seemed to be a new interpretation of an old rule. She was insistent. "You could take a *minute* to call me, couldn't you? And by the way, what the other girls do is not important to me. *You* are the one who's important, and that's why I'm making an issue out of this."

As often happens, the mother and daughter didn't enter

immediately into the negotiating process. Emotions were too intense. Each person was convinced she could try to bulldoze the other verbally and succeed in getting her own way. But the arguments kept going around and around in a circle, with no resolution in sight.

Clearly the mother had made a mistake. She had opened the conversation with an accusation, and this approach caused Ann to react defensively. As a result, neither person was able to listen to the other calmly.

The problem didn't go away. Ann continued to take her ballet lessons—and she continued to be late on occasion. Finally the mother saw that the best way to resolve the issue would be to try genuine negotiation. So, drawing on some of her past experience in the bargaining process, she began by setting a positive tone.

"Ann, I get very concerned when you're late from ballet class," the mother said. "Let's try to work it out. Is there any way you could let me know when you're going to be late? You know how I worry when I don't know where you are."

Ann responded much more maturely to this approach. As a result the mother got much more helpful information, upon which a mutually agreeable settlement could be based. For one thing, Ann explained in more detail why she couldn't interrupt her class to make a phone call. "There are really no breaks in the lesson anymore. I can't leave, even for a minute or so," Ann said. "Lessons last longer than they used to. If I walk out of the class—especially toward the end when the teacher is talking about some important points—I'll miss out on the most important part of the instruction.

"Also, sometimes the teacher lets the class run too long, without giving us any advance warning," Ann continued. "Again, I suppose I could just walk out, but I'd miss so much!"

The mother decided she would have to accept this argument. After all, she was the one who was paying for the ballet lessons, not her daughter. She certainly wanted to be sure that she got her money's worth!

Part of the problem also lay in the fact that Ann wasn't always so considerate of her mother's feelings. Mom understood this, and she realized it would help if she found a way to make her daughter's dilemma less painful. "Maybe I could speak to your teacher about providing a short break so that those who need to can make a phone call toward the end of the class," her mother suggested.

"That would be just fine with me," Ann replied. "There are always three or four other girls who are in the same position I'm in, always feeling pressed because their parents worry about them."

"Now, if I talk to your teacher about this, will you do something for me?" her mother asked.

"What's that?"

"You come along with me, to explain that *you* also want a break. That way the burden of explaining to the teacher won't be all on me. If I go in alone, she'll think I'm being an unreasonable, overprotective parent because she knows I worry about you when you don't get home on time. If you go with me, that would set my mind more at ease."

The mother also assured Ann that in asking for the call, she wasn't implying that she didn't trust the girl or that she felt Ann was immature or unable to take care of herself. Quite the contrary, the mother was proud of how grown-up and responsible her teenager had become.

Ann was sympathetic, but she wanted a little more latitude in the time when she would make the call. Finally, the two of them agreed that if Ann was going to be more than a half hour late, she'd let her mother know.

This arrangement succeeded and worked out quite well

for several months. Then, as Ann passed her sixteenth birthday, the mother felt it was appropriate for her to become more independent—and so she made another change in the negotiation. She dropped the requirement that Ann call. But in this case, Ann continued to do so!

In short, the phone-call problem was no longer an issue. The main difficulty had been that the girl was moving through a transition period in the maturing process, and the mother wasn't keeping up. The parent had felt a need to keep more control than the daughter believed was warranted. By talking the problem through, the mother and daughter were able to come to a better understanding of one another's thinking. And they arrived at a series of settlements acceptable to both.

This is a classic example of how a parent must learn to "loosen the reins" as a child nears adulthood. In turn a youngster must learn to be respectful of a parent's concern for her welfare, even when the child has reached a relatively advanced age. Agreements like the one outlined here avoid coercion, anger, or hostility, and they leave the reservoirs of family love undrained.

In this case, Ann felt somewhat in danger of being smothered by her mother's attentiveness. On the other hand, the mother was fearful that the girl was not ready to become independent of her family moorings. The object of the negotiation was to establish a balance between these seemingly contradictory concerns.

Tactic 6. Consider using an impartial third party as mediator.

Sometimes negotiations don't get off the ground because a particular parent is the wrong person to try to work out a deal with a particular problem. Often this is because feelings about the problem have run too high, and calm discussions seem to be impossible. At such times, the parent who's having the problem should consider bringing in another adult, in effect a "third-party mediator," to conduct the negotiations.

One mother had always been anxious about her eleven-year-old son when he had to cross a busy avenue on his regular trips to a local park. Another youngster had been struck down and killed by a car while riding a bicycle along this thoroughfare, and the eleven-year-old's mother had asked her son never to ride his bicycle on *or* across this avenue. He agreed to walk his bike instead of riding it when he went across or on the avenue, as long as he would still be allowed to go to the park, and that had seemed all right to the mother. In fact, this arrangement worked for a few weeks.

But one day when the mother was out shopping, she spotted her son riding—not walking—his bike across the very same avenue that they had discussed! She was furious! Still fuming when the boy arrived home, she berated him for disobeying her and for reneging on their agreement. The angry argument escalated to the point where neither the mother nor the son was able to discuss the matter rationally. Finally, desperate for help, the mother turned to the father for assistance.

Acting in effect as a third-party mediator, the father first called the boy into the kitchen and asked him to sit down for a man-to-man discussion. "Your mother saw you riding your bike across the avenue this afternoon," the father began. "Why didn't you walk it across, as you had agreed?" The boy was reluctant to answer at first. But the father pressed ahead gently: "If you tell me why, I may be able to help you work out something with your mother."

Saying why wasn't easy. The boy didn't offer any believable reasons for his strong feelings about the issue. Finally the father had a stroke of brilliance: He asked if the other boys had kidded the youngster when he walked the bicycle across the street.

Eventually the boy admitted that having to walk his bike across the avenue made him "feel like a baby." And some of his friends had laughed at his caution as they sped ahead of him across the street.

The explanation seemed valid to the father, and with this important piece of information in hand, he asked the mother to join the discussion. The three spent some time talking about their fears and feelings about the dangerous street. The father, as the mediator, made it a point not to take sides. He kept very calm, even as the mother and son occasionally expressed their frustrations.

After they had aired all sides of the issue, the father offered some evaluations. First of all, he said that he agreed with the mother that the thoroughfare was extremely dangerous. To make the point, he cited several instances of accidents on the thoroughfare, in addition to the death of the other boy on the bicycle. For that matter, the son agreed that the street was one of the most dangerous places in their neighborhood.

On the other hand, the father openly sympathized with the boy about his desire to be "one of the guys." The father mentioned some instances from his own childhood in which he had had similar experiences and feelings.

But how could they balance these two conflicting considerations? That was the question the father put on the table, and the three of them then began to discuss it.

As mediator, the father had managed to get an agreement on some of the basic facts that had to be known before a negotiated settlement. He had also framed the main issue they had to resolve. Finally he set a calm, rational tone that paved the way to a mutually agreeable deal.

The three of them reached the following understanding:

1. The boy would never ride his bike *on*—that is up or down—the street.

2. The boy would *always* come to a full stop on his bicycle when he reached the busy street.

3. He could ride his bike across the street if he first stopped and carefully checked to be certain that no cars were coming from either direction.

The parents agreed to this third point after considering these two factors:

• After thinking about it, the mother realized that riding the bike across the street would get the boy across faster. He would thus be exposed to danger for a shorter period of time, as long as he was careful with the traffic.

• Finally, by allowing the boy to exercise some discretion in riding his bike across the street, they recognized his increasing maturity.

4. The father agreed to help the boy develop some "comebacks" to respond to the criticisms of his peers. With the means to answer when he was ridiculed, the boy felt he could take the criticism better.

The father capped this successful negotiation with some advice to his son about peer pressure. He said, "You know, we're still asking you to be more cautious than some of your classmates. But that's because we think your classmates are being foolhardy about the way they use their bicycles. Even many *adults* wouldn't ride on that street—your mother and I certainly wouldn't!"

Some risks, the father emphasized, are worth taking. Others are nothing but foolish, dangerous posturing. "Some soldiers or fighter pilots will take chances that they know they have to take—and they are recognized as courageous because of their actions. But they wouldn't take chances by driving their cars at a hundred miles an hour in a thirty-mile-an-hour zone!" the father said.

The son agreed with this argument—and it gave him some verbal ammunition to use with friends who might make fun of him for his relative caution with his bicycle.

Clearly a cool, calm third party can be a major factor in putting a family discussion back on an even keel!

Tactic 7. Establish an atmosphere where you can really listen to your child.

Effective bargaining begins when you get the other party to open up to you. It's important to be sure you're calm enough to be frank about your feelings without becoming hostile or emotional. And of course you have to pay close attention to what your child is saying—and what *you* are saying. It isn't always easy to get your child to talk during a negotiation, and sometimes the major obstacle can lie in the way you respond to your child.

You have to be careful to begin in a calm and reasonable way and to maintain that attitude throughout the discussions —as we discussed in the Principles of Positive Persuasion. Be alert to hostility, ridicule, sarcasm, and accusations. These will poison any discussion. And don't try to assign blame or bring in past lapses or other bad behavior. If a child gets defensive, he'll clam up and you won't have a negotiation.

If your youngster is slow to speak, be persistent but gentle in coaxing out of him what he really thinks and feels about the issue. And when he finally does say something, listen respectfully, without making fun or belittling him.

In the bicycle example that we've just considered, you'll notice that the father approached his son in a straightforward manner and encouraged open, honest communications. He was really listening to his youngster in a way that gave the boy confidence that the final result would be fair and even-handed. One thing that the father did *not* do was to give his son an opportunity to lie by asking the boy *if* he had ridden his bike across the avenue. He wisely avoided setting a trap for his son that would have led to an angry confrontation. Instead he started out by stating that he knew the mother had seen the boy riding across the avenue in the afternoon.

If the child had been given the opportunity to lie—or had not been given access to all the facts that the parent had— the father would have been trying to win an advantage in the negotiation, one that would have been resented. These games are unworthy of honest negotiators. If the boy had been caught in a fib, he would have become wary, close-mouthed, and perhaps even hostile. He would have known his father had not really been willing to listen to him, but had been playing verbal games in which the main goal was to try to get the upper hand.

Remember: You have to establish an environment in which your child feels comfortable discussing his or her deepest feelings with you. Even if your child doesn't keep to the reasonable and calm atmosphere you want for the negotiations, you must be especially careful to do so yourself. If you meet angry accusations with similar reactions of your own, you'll block communication, and all your attempts at listening will be in vain.

Tactic 8. Keep cool.

All negative emotions, including anger, can be very destructive when you're trying to develop an atmosphere conducive to negotiation.

Popular thinking has usually presented anger as a force like steam in a pipe: If you don't let the steam out, the pipe will burst. This old idea dies hard. But research indicates that angry behaviors are more like a fire that feeds on itself and produces other fires nearby. Anger and aggression are likely to provoke a similar response, and a vicious cycle of ploy and counterploy, coercion and rebellion, results.

This helps to explain what happens when you argue with your children. One mother received a call from school that her son had misbehaved, and she confronted him angrily when he arrived home. "Your principal called me up today and told me you were throwing food in the lunchroom!" she shouted. "What's the matter with you? How many times have I told you to behave yourself in school?"

Here the mother's anger has emerged as a loud accusation, intended to hurt but not designed to get information (despite the questions she had asked). Predictably the child became quite defensive. "You always blame me! You never ask for my side of the story! It wasn't my fault. I didn't start it! I always get blamed for everything!"

The child's response is just what Mom should have expected, and the result was that they were getting nowhere. A major argument was off and running, with very few facts on the table. Feelings escalated, and the initial bursts of anger quickly careened out of control. In less than five minutes, this mother and son were "going at each other's throats."

Because of the possibility of such catastrophic confrontations, I don't think it's ever useful to ventilate anger to your children. Anger is an emotion we probably can't help feeling. But expressing it directly is seldom to your advantage in the home. When you force reluctant cooperation from your children with angry outbursts, you'll tend to pay for any temporary gains you get with losses in cooperation, respect, and love.

When people are angry, they tend to think in terms of retaliation. They want to hurt; they want to exact revenge. Such feelings on the part of parents loose similar reactions in their child and help create a dangerous atmosphere that can easily result in enduring scars on their relationship.

So always try to bypass angry feelings when you're negotiating. As your negotiations progress, your anger will give way to satisfaction. If you're frustrated or upset, it's all right to *say* you feel this way; but don't express it in shouting or derogatory remarks.

Some people object to this viewpoint. They say anger is a "natural" and common reaction. But often such people seem to be looking for ways to justify their own reactions they can't control. Perhaps the popularity of the "let it all hang out" idea is nothing more than an attempt to justify the inability to avoid expressing anger and other negative emotions. Some people even enjoy the power hostile expressions can give them. But such satisfactions have no place in a happy home.

Still the main question remains: Are there any techniques for putting a cap on your anger? In fact there are. First you should learn to recognize behavior and reactions that are associated with the buildup of anger. I find it helpful just to step back, almost as though you're stepping outside of your body, and take a good look at what you are doing as a result of your anger. Watch what you are saying to yourself, what you are saying to others, and what you are doing. And see how other people are reacting to you.

Listen to your thoughts. Note how you tend to blow your child's faults out of proportion. See how thoughts of retaliation and punishment run through your mind. Check how you begin to dredge up old faults and transgressions that the child has committed. Your anger may come out in punitive demands, deprivations, or physical punishments. Or you may find yourself unwilling to open up at all to your child for fear of the outbursts that a direct confrontation may cause.

To detect the results of your anger, look closely at your child. See how angry expressions cause him to wilt, to retire, or to retaliate in such a way as to irritate or anger you even more. If you can just step back and look at what's happening in you and in your youngster—and how you are hurting and being unfair to him—that should help to defuse some of your anger.

At this point you need to withdraw and plan a more constructive response. Try a calm, cool, reasonable negotiation —an approach that should be the best tonic of all.

In any event, as I've mentioned before, I think it's best to avoid any attempts at negotiation when you're in an angry state. Just stop the discussion and postpone it to a time when you can approach the matter more calmly.

As these tactics demonstrate, it's not always so easy to conduct an effective negotiation with your child. But if you keep some of these practical techniques of give-and-take in mind as you approach a discussion, you'll find that many problems can be avoided.

There's still another key negotiating tactic that must be mentioned. Up to this point, the negotiating sessions we've described have been entirely oral. The offers, counteroffers, and settlements are simple enough to be stated out loud, and all parties involved know exactly what's expected. But sometimes, especially with older children, negotiations can get so complicated—and the settlements so detailed—that it's easy to misinterpret or forget what was said or agreed upon during a negotiating session. To prevent this, it's important on these occasions for parents and children to commit their deals to writing.

4.

Should You Put It in Writing?

"*B*UT, Mom, you promised!"

How often have you heard your child make this charge? And how often have you wondered, "Is she right? Did I *really* promise?"

Parents frequently find themselves in the position of having to justify or defend things they have said or allegedly said. Most parents don't purposely lie to their children. But many times, it's hard, if not impossible, to remember exactly what was agreed to in a conversation days or even weeks in the past. This can put an adult in a very uncomfortable position and cause him to make excuses like, "I never *meant* that if you finished up all your homework you could go out *every* school night!" Or, "I may have said you could wear makeup when you go out on weekends, but that *didn't* mean that you can wear it to school!"

Such scenes occur frequently in American family life, with either Mom or Dad winding up as the culprit who is—or *seems* to be—the big "promise breaker." And more often than not, the main problem is that oral agreements have been stated too imprecisely. Or key parts of those agree-

74

ments have been completely forgotten by one party or the other.

I can remember an incident in my own childhood when I had just such a misunderstanding with my father. I had wanted a puppy almost as far back as I could remember; every Christmas and birthday I'd beg my parents for one. Partly to stop my pestering, my father, who didn't like dogs, said I could have a puppy—but only when I was old enough to undertake full responsibility for its care.

At this point memories begin to get fuzzy. Somewhere along the line as the months and years went by, I decided that he had promised me that I could have a puppy when I was ten years old. So on the weekend before my tenth birthday, I suggested that maybe we should start looking for a puppy before it was too late. My dad looked at me in astonishment and declared, "What do you mean, a puppy?"

In the ensuing conversation—argument would be a better word—he vowed that he had never promised me a puppy for my tenth birthday. I responded with such anger and hurt that I can still feel those emotions coursing through my being, even after all these years.

In protest, I stayed in my room for the entire Saturday before my birthday. I refused to eat and sobbed inconsolably. Although my mother tried to reason with me, I wouldn't talk or even listen to her. My heart was broken; at some deep level, I felt betrayed by my own father. And, though I didn't recognize it, I was hoping my misery would persuade him to give in. Finally he *did* give in. On Sunday he agreed to get me a dog, and peace was restored.

Who was right and who was wrong?

I honestly don't know—and I don't believe this is the right question to ask. In considering how to conduct effective negotiations, we're not at all concerned with the art of assigning blame. I hope my father never regretted or resented having given that dog to me, but there's no doubt about one thing: We had gotten involved in a misunderstanding that need not have occurred if only we had possessed some means of keeping our facts straight.

When a parent who usually keeps promises doesn't do so, or even seems not to do so, the child's emotional response may be extreme. Furthermore, the child's intense disappointment often causes the parent to make compensation in some way. A system of emotional blackmail can easily develop in such circumstances. Children learn at extremely young ages that their emotions can influence their parents— and almost all youngsters make use of this knowledge!

To put this another way, children's emotions, after they pass infancy, are seldom entirely just automatic responses to pain or happiness. Rather they often also involve some form of social coercion. Without being at all conscious of it, children learn that even minor discomforts or wants, if expressed with enough force, can be quite effective tools. But they are certainly not among the tools we advocate.

In short, a youngster's emotions may signal a couple of important messages that should be understood before negotiation gets under way:

1. I feel strongly and I want such-and-such badly; and
2. Until I get it, we're both going to be miserable!

These messages may well be involved when your child's emotions seem out of control. But it's also important to realize that such childish coercion isn't healthy. It's much better for children to learn other ways to work out problems.

When you promise your child something, that promise should be clearly understood. If unspoken conditions are included in the promise, they should be explained in detail.

Even after you've offered your explanation, I think it's wise to ask, "Now, do you understand what I've said?"

Even if the child indicates an understanding, it's still usually wise to ask him to *rephrase* his perception of the agreement in his own words. Otherwise you may find later that a child's nodded agreement didn't mean as much as you thought. The two of you may not have been on the same wavelength.

When your child has lived up to an agreement, it's up to you to uphold your end of the bargain as well. If you renege in any way, you'll be laying the groundwork for big trouble. Most devastating of all, your child may begin to question the trust and faith that he should place in the negotiating tactics you are trying to teach.

No matter how hard a parent and child try, oral agreements are likely to fall short. One party or the other may forget, misunderstand, or try to undermine the agreement. That is why I suggest that on important, complex issues, it's best to 1) write out your agreement, and 2) call it what it is —a contract. If you hope to keep things interesting for your youngster, contracts should not be couched in turgid legalese. Instead, use everyday language, including plenty of your child's own thoughts and phrases.

Some parents shudder at the idea of being so "cold" or "businesslike" as to draw up a written agreement with their child. "That's much too formal for my taste," some may object. "I prefer to rely on love and trust to work things out rather than some sort of legalistic written agreement."

But think about it for a moment. We've already seen how trust, love, and all the other wonderful qualities of a good parent-child relationship can be jeopardized by misunderstandings in oral promises and agreements. So, on a purely practical level, if you put it in writing, you may actually find that you *enhance* the trust and love in your relationship with your child.

You'll likely find your child is pleased to be treated in such an adult way. Not only that, you'll discover that the process of writing out an agreement can be a lot of fun. It also will be educational for your child, especially if he writes it out himself. I encourage you to get your youngster to draft as much of the agreement as he can. The challenge of organizing his thoughts and putting them down on paper will provide invaluable self-instruction in basic verbal skills.

There are other benefits of this process that reach far beyond the life of any child-parent contract. A series of written agreements over a number of years can provide a record of happy memories for you and your children after they're grown up. A file of these agreements can become as important and enjoyable a part of those early years as old photographs and letters.

To understand the circumstances under which a written contract will work, it's helpful to see how the principle operates in practice. So now let's turn to an incident involving an acquaintance of mine. A man I know had three daughters, aged twelve, fifteen, and seventeen. He also had a big problem a couple of years ago—the family telephone.

Some nights neither he nor his wife could receive a call. If the father wanted to call someone, he had to order one of his daughters off the telephone. The three sisters fought constantly among themselves over whose turn it was to use the telephone, and none of the girls was gracious enough to relinquish it without a fight.

There was the perennial problem of his sky-high telephone bill; every time he got one, he got angry. Once the father became so enraged that he tore the kitchen phone out of the wall! This man had always been quite easygoing. But the problem with the telephone had really gotten to him.

When he calmed down, he realized that violence wasn't the answer. But he had to do something. So he decided to have all the telephone extensions in the home removed except the one in the kitchen. He thought the lack of privacy would discourage lengthy conversations. But he was wrong. The girls simply gravitated toward the kitchen phone, whispered over it in low tones, and squabbled with the same intensity as before.

I became aware of this problem when the man called my office and left a message. I tried several times to return his call but, as you might expect, I couldn't get through. I finally called him at his office, and that's when I heard more about the size of the home-telephone problem. As simple as it might sound to an outsider, it was making this man's domestic life miserable. So when he asked for help, I began to explore some possibilities with him.

My first suggestion: "Why don't you get the girls a phone of their own?"

"Absolutely not!" he replied. "They're spoiled enough already. Besides, I have two sons in college. Another phone would cost too much. I never had such a luxury when I was growing up. One telephone is enough for any family!"

Clearly he wasn't in the mood for a simple solution. So I made a few suggestions that I hoped would get him in the mood for negotiating. "Obviously, you haven't been able to come up with an answer to this problem by yourself, so we need to do some creative thinking," I said, and he grudgingly agreed. "I could suggest some other possible solutions, but I'm convinced that they would never work in your family unless *everyone* agrees to them," I continued. "In other

79

words, you and I can't sit here and come up with a good idea without getting your wife and daughters involved."

"So what *do* you suggest?" he replied.

Even though his tone wasn't altogether friendly, this was the opening I'd been looking for. His attitude signaled that we were nearing the point where true negotiations could begin. You have to be *willing* to work together with the other side for a mutually agreeable settlement.

In his case, I didn't have to avoid the word *negotiation,* as is sometimes necessary when dealing with those who might be scared away by a relatively formal term. This man was a plant manager and was quite familiar with the use of negotiating tactics in labor relationships. I did have to point out, however, that dealing with your family is quite different from dealing with management.

In ordinary labor negotiations, one side usually tries to get an advantage over the other. With a family, the objectives are different. The idea here should be *not* to get an advantage, but to create a context and reach a solution in which each participant can express his love and respect for the others. It may be necessary for the side with the most power (the parents) to give way to the weaker parties (the children). Only an approach such as this can offer hope for coming up with a long-term, mutually satisfying solution.

This tied-up-telephone situation presented some especially difficult problems. For one thing, there were many more people involved than in most parent-child negotiations. Three daughters, the father, and the mother all had to reach an understanding, because each was a user of the telephone.

Because of the complexity of this negotiation, I suggested at the outset that any final settlement should be written out and that each party should sign the agreement. That way there could be no misunderstanding about the ultimate provisions.

The basic concept seemed reasonable to the father. So we put our heads together to work out an initial offer that might appeal to the children. In the first place, he suspected that they would be concerned if they realized just how terrible this telephone situation was making him feel. So they would probably be quite willing to help solve the problem.

Accordingly we worked out an initial offer for him to make to his family. The girls would be allowed to use the telephone twenty minutes each day. But they couldn't make any calls or receive any after 9:00 P.M. on weekdays. On weekends and holidays they would be allowed thirty minutes per day each, the time to be divided along certain lines suggested by the parents. But they would still have to abide by the no-calls-after-9:00-P.M. rule. And they would have to pay for telephone use on any call that lasted more than ten minutes to the same person.

This offer sounded reasonable to me. But I also suggested that he regard these proposals *only* as proposals because they would probably have to be changed in the course of negotiations.

Being a seasoned negotiator himself, the father quickly agreed to give it a try, and he took steps to set up a negotiating session and get things moving. That very evening he called the family together, explained the concept of negotiating, and laid out the terms of his initial offer.

Everyone in the family was fascinated with the idea. They were all intelligent and loved to discuss practically anything. But as I had warned him, the father found he needed to be flexible. No one was willing to go along completely with his initial offer.

Fortunately everyone kept all negative feelings in check.

The girls were sympathetic when their father told them how miserable their behavior had been making him. So at the outset they were motivated to seek a solution to the problem, just as he was.

But the girls had their own ideas about the way the final settlement should be shaped. None objected much to the idea of paying a small amount from her earnings or allowance for extended use of the phone, but the twenty-minute limitation was a problem. Still, the father insisted that some limitation was essential because he just had to have the phone free for part of each evening.

The oldest, the seventeen-year-old, argued that her more developed dating life and high-school activities should entitle her to more time than twenty minutes per night on the telephone. Predictably this caused the fifteen-year-old to counter, "So you think your activities and your friends are more important than mine? That's crazy!"

The twelve-year-old didn't think she should be a second- or third-class citizen either, and she said so. It seemed an impasse might be in the offing.

But then the father helped to open things up: "Okay, just remember now I want us to reach a solution that's going to be acceptable to *everybody*. But if the three of you can't agree on anything, then we may just have to forget the telephone completely."

That rather negative proposal perhaps shouldn't have been offered. Threats of catastrophic actions are hardly ever helpful in a negotiation. But at this point, the mother stepped in with a suggestion. "What do you say that each of you would have the right to talk the same amount of time?" she said. "But maybe there could be some adjustments about the time of day when you would talk, depending on age, social activities, and so forth."

"My boyfriend really can't talk until after he's through with football practice and supper," the seventeen-year-old quickly replied. "That means about eight or eight-thirty. So I'd rather talk to him and my girlfriends in the evening."

"I'd like to use it after supper too, but eight o'clock is all right with me," the fifteen-year-old said.

"I'll take the afternoon," the twelve-year-old said—and that settled at least part of the problem.

The oldest girl jumped in again: "You know, I really need more time than twenty minutes. Sometimes I have to go over a tough math problem with one of my friends. That can take ten minutes before you've even started."

"Me, too," the other children said.

So now the ball was back in the parents' court. As a good negotiator should, the father asked them for a counteroffer: "So how much time do you think you need?" he asked.

The girls thought for a minute. They sensed quite correctly that if they got too far beyond twenty minutes they might overplay their hand.

"How about thirty minutes?" the fifteen-year-old suggested.

"That would be okay," the eldest agreed.

"Yes, thirty minutes," the youngest said.

But now, it was the mother's turn: "That's a lot of time. If there were just one of you, that might be fine. But with three, that means the phone will be tied up an hour and a half each day! I think that's too much."

"I have had people tell me they tried to get me for several days, but the phone was always busy," the father said. "Still, I know you girls have a high need to use the phone. So let's see if we can work something out."

After a while they all concurred that the most active time of the day for incoming calls was usually from about eight o'clock on. But unfortunately, that was exactly the time when the two oldest girls wanted to tie up the phone.

Finally they all agreed that thirty minutes would be acceptable. But the two oldest girls would be allowed a maximum of fifteen minutes each between eight and nine o'clock on weekdays. They would have to use their other fifteen minutes earlier in the day. Each daughter also would be allowed an extra ten minutes on the phone on Saturday and Sunday.

The mother was appointed to be in charge of timekeeping. She set up a self-recording scheme, whereby the girls would keep track of their telephone usage with a common pad and pencil. Finally the father and mother made the settlement dependent on the girls' ability to negotiate among themselves for their respective uses of the phone. They had to agree about any exchanges of times that they might want to make.

The final written agreement looked like this:

TELEPHONE USE

Agreed

For Alice and Betty [the eldest children] calls are limited to 30 minutes total on weekdays. No more than 15 minutes total after 8:00 P.M. No calls after 9 o'clock P.M.

For Carolle [youngest] same as for Alice and Betty, but must hang up by 8:00 P.M.

After 9:00 P.M., if either parent is home, calls out by children are for emergencies only. Such calls out are to be placed by the parents and to be supervised by them. Only parents can answer the phone after 9:00 P.M. If neither parent is home, calls out are still for emergencies only, and incoming calls must be very brief—callers should be asked to call at another time.

The beginning and ending times for all calls, and also the person being called, are to be recorded on the pad by the phone and signed.

Each of the two older girls will be charged 3 cents per minute for any conversation over 10 minutes, with the same party on the same day. Carolle will be charged 2 cents per minute for the same time periods.

Children can change times by agreement, but no coercion or arguments are permitted.

On weekends, all times are extended by 10 minutes, but no time on the phone is permitted after 9:00 P.M. Parents agree to permit use of two extension phones while the agreement is kept by the children. Violations will result in further negotiations. Negotiations will be reopened after one month to check for the effectiveness of this agreement.

[Signed]
Alice: _____
Betty: _____
Carolle: _____
Mom: _____
Dad: _____

This system worked out beautifully, and peace finally began to reign again in this family. It was now possible to reach the father consistently on the phone after 9:00 P.M.!

Of course there were rough spots in the agreement that had to be worked out as time went on. The youngest girl found that she sometimes wanted to use the phone *after* eight o'clock, but the agreement that she had signed didn't allow that. As a result, a few months later, it was necessary to work out an amendment to the contract to give her a little more flexibility.

For the amendment to be effective, each person who had signed the original contract had to agree to the change. So the youngest girl faced some nerve-racking moments as she wondered whether everyone would agree to her suggestions.

Another problem was that the timekeeping procedure didn't go along too smoothly or accurately. The mother and father didn't stand over the girls with a stopwatch, and so sometimes there were disputes about who had talked how long. But in general the girls were able to work out their mutual problems and also limit their phone use to suit their parents' needs.

On the whole, the negotiating process had worked quite well. Perhaps most important of all, these three children had learned some key things that would certainly prove useful to them later in life. Among the most significant of these lessons:

• Problems can be solved if they're discussed in a reasonable manner.

• Language can be used as a tool to explain precisely what you mean.

• If any group is to function together happily, each member of the group must listen carefully to the complaints of others and must be considerate of others' rights.

• A contract should be read carefully before it is signed.

• A contract is binding unless the other signers agree to a change.

If you have to learn some hard lessons about the power of written contracts, a loving family is the best school. If a child makes a mistake, for instance, and signs his name to a contract that's not in his own best interests, an understanding family won't usually hold him to it.

But still, even in a family, there will be some gentle pressure to think things through and be very careful about what you sign. And if a child makes a mistake, that can provide a good object lesson. He'll get some idea about the bad things that might happen if he becomes careless in a similar situation in the outside world.

In the final analysis, however, love and respect are the motivations that make negotiations work in a family setting. This is such an important point that I think it can't be over-emphasized. In the case of the negotiation we've just considered, things went relatively smoothly because the daughters loved the father and realized they were upsetting him. They wanted to serve their own self-interests, but at the same time they wanted to change their behavior to please their parent.

Unless you've alienated your children completely, their love is one of the most important assets you have on your side during a negotiating session. The vast majority of children want to please their parents, *if* they can do so at a reasonable cost. This is true even of teenagers who may seem to be completely indifferent to adult sensitivities.

To break through the façade and get your kids working with you, it's important to give them opportunities to express their love. More often than not, the best way to open them up is to open yourself up. You might tell them, "You know I really love you and I'm unhappy about the fact that we can't seem to get along together on this issue."

Believe me, such an opening, if it is accompanied by a sincere show of respect for the child's wishes, can go a long way toward melting even the hardest adolescent heart. Still, verbal affirmations of affection have to be backed up by action in the form of visible benefits for the child. At least one such benefit—the use of the telephone—was hanging in the balance in the negotiation we've just discussed. Harmony in the household was clearly involved as well.

As we've seen, when such benefits get complex and hard

to administer, the arrangement should be put into writing. A written document can sometimes be the most effective way of saying to your child, "I care about you, and I want to be sure you get everything you're entitled to."

One special type of arrangement, which often demands the use of a written contract, has become a staple of negotiated settlements between parents and children. This kind of deal is based on what has come to be known as the "token system."

5.

How to Seal a Deal with the Token System

*S*OMETIMES, especially with very young children, consequences for good behavior can be very simple. Parental approval and affection are often the most important rewards. Beyond that a star, a sticker, or a cheap toy may be just the thing to help motivate a youngster to better his behavior.

But as children get older, you give them more difficult assignments and expect them to master tougher skills and show more independence. Negotiated agreements may accumulate, and rewards become more complex. One of the most effective ways to manage more sophisticated rewards and to close a negotiation with your child successfully is to establish a "token system." It may help to think about this approach in terms of setting up a simple family "money system."

In general, token systems involve the use of some tangible item called a "token" to signify to your child that he has done something the two of you have agreed upon. In other words, you may give your youngster a poker chip, a star, a check mark, or a numerical point score every time he lives up to his part of the bargain. These are the "tokens" that signal the child's achievement.

When the youngster has accumulated a sufficient number of these tokens, he can exchange them for rewards, which might be toys, the use of the family car, or other benefits. Thus the tokens make pleasurable certain tasks that may otherwise seem onerous to the child. As he should, he will feel that cooperation with parental wishes is not a one-way street.

Token systems are especially helpful when you and your child have resolved a negotiation with an agreement that permits the youngster to earn larger rewards, or some that can't be given immediately or frequently. To illustrate in specific terms how this works, let's take a look at how tokens helped a little girl to get out of bed in the morning.

Mrs. Jones, who had recently been through a difficult divorce, was just beginning to pull her life together again. She had gotten a good job and had succeeded in setting up a fairly smooth-running, single-parent household.

But she had a problem. Her ten-year-old daughter Sandy wouldn't get out of bed in the morning.

Every morning at 7:00 A.M., Mrs. Jones would call Sandy, but the girl would pull the covers over her head and refuse to emerge. Several calls and a visit to the bedroom were regularly required. When Sandy finally got up, she delayed getting dressed, fussing over her clothes, and frequently being late for the bus to school.

This behavior was especially exasperating because the mother also had a younger child, a son, whom she also had to get ready in time for the school bus every morning. And she herself had to get to work after the children had gone.

The mother couldn't afford to have Sandy miss the bus and have to be driven to school. So every day the pressure would build as she tried to manage her many morning chores while screaming at Sandy, "Quit fooling around and get out of that bedroom!"

By the time Mrs. Jones got in touch with me to help solve this and other problems with her daughter, she was frantic. "I never thought I'd see the day when I couldn't handle my own ten-year-old daughter!" she told me. "Please help me."

She was especially worried about the effect her divorce might have had on her daughter. But I advised her not to get into any deep "psychologizing." Feeling guilty would not help her. The difficulty to be confronted, I assured her, was in the actual behavior, including the negative interactions she and her daughter were having.

We discussed ways to make the mornings, and the rest of the day, more pleasant for Sandy. We also explored how Mrs. Jones could change from her nervous, hectoring style to an approach that would include more praise and affection.

"Just focus on Sandy's behavior, and your behavior—on what you want changed," I said.

Then I asked Mrs. Jones if she would be willing to negotiate with Sandy, and she agreed. I decided to be present at the first negotiating session as an impartial third party, because I sensed that these two might need some help bridging the communications gap that had developed between them.

As it happened, Mrs. Jones needed all the help she could get. At our first meeting, we didn't make any progress at all.

"Sandy, when you don't get out of bed in the morning, it makes things difficult for all of us, don't you think?" the mother began.

But Sandy didn't respond. In fact, she just looked down at the floor.

"If I'm late for work, I'll lose my job—that wouldn't be so great, would it?" Mrs. Jones continued.

Still, silence. Mrs. Jones had discouraged communication. Sandy felt she was being blamed for her mother's difficulties at work and at home.

"Your brother doesn't want to be late for school, and it isn't good for you to be late, either," the mother said. "Is there anything I can do for you that will make getting up any easier?"

This time Sandy shook her head, but she still wouldn't speak.

"Do you want me to help you pick out your clothes the night before?" Mrs. Jones asked.

She was beginning to try out some ways to change the situation that Sandy faced in the morning. Of course, part of that situation was the mother's anxious rush to get her ready for school—an attitude that created a generally unpleasant atmosphere. The mother felt that if Sandy would only be efficient and quick, they would start getting along well. But Sandy obviously hadn't been able to meet this requirement.

"Do you need me to help you check to see if you have everything you need before you leave for school?"

More silence.

"Would you rather have your own alarm clock, so that you could get up by yourself?"

The girl shook her head again, but still no verbal response.

In the next few minutes, Mrs. Jones tried everything we had arranged for her to suggest, and everything else she could possibly think of. But still she got no reply. Sandy would only occasionally shake her head no to each of her mother's suggestions. She obviously wasn't interested in getting involved in any sort of give-and-take.

Realizing that we had reached a major impasse before we even got started, I intervened: "Maybe you'd like to spend a little time thinking about this problem of getting up in the morning, Sandy. Then, we'll get together next Thursday and discuss it again. How about that?"

Sandy shrugged her shoulders, but she still didn't say anything. It seemed best for both the mother and me just to back off and let the idea of negotiating sink into the girl's thinking for a few days. Then we could try again.

Although I remained optimistic about the possibility of changing things, I realized that Sandy's lack of cooperation wasn't the only problem. The negative quality of the interaction between mother and daughter needed to change as well. But my efforts hadn't borne any more fruit than had the mother's during this first session. I still thought I should continue to be a third party in the negotiation. A mediator, such as a therapist, or more likely a cool-headed parent, relative, or friend, can help to inhibit bursts of anger on both sides. Hostility will destroy the atmosphere that's necessary for a successful negotiation. In this situation, I feared that unless I stayed involved, Mrs. Jones might get so frustrated that she would try to negotiate by using her bad old ways of dealing with her daughter.

It would also have been very tempting for this mother—or any other parent in her situation—to resort to the use of punishment to get Sandy up and ready for school on time. Unfortunately parents too often learn how well punishments, if severe enough, can achieve an immediate objective. When the Godfather of the recent film talked about making someone an offer he couldn't refuse, he wasn't talking about a bribe, but about something Godfather types find even more effective—threats of terrible punishment to come!

But in the home, punishment would have created more problems than it could solve. Relations between mother and daughter couldn't be improved by it. Fortunately my presence made Sandy's mother more inclined to exhaust the other possible solutions first. Somehow the girl had to be motivated by positive means. Although gentle persuasion and praise seemed unlikely to succeed by themselves, they were certainly going to be essential components of any solution.

The next day I got in touch with Mrs. Jones and suggested that she think of some reward or prize that might be particularly attractive to Sandy. Sandy could then earn the reward by getting up on time in the morning. She would also have a chance to experience Mrs. Jones's more positive style—and, we hoped, Mrs. Jones would have a chance to practice it.

The mother had trouble coming up with a concept at first. The only thing that Mrs. Jones had heard Sandy talk with any excitement about recently was the prospect of visiting her grandmother in Florida. But this had seemed too expensive a proposition, and so the mother had to discard the idea.

We thought instead about some other, less extravagant local trips. Sandy liked to ice skate, and occasionally her mom would take her out to a charming country rink or give her the bus fare and ticket price. This looked like a way we might break through Sandy's negative attitude and get her moving in the morning. But since skating was at most a once-a-week affair, the key to making the concept work would be the establishment of an intermediate reward—a token system.

To reiterate, the basic idea is that if a child cooperates with a parent and does what is expected, she'll receive a token. Tokens are substitutes for something of value—just as in our nation's money system. When you set up a token system, you and your child agree that a given number of tokens can be exchanged for some reward.

In other words, a child may earn a colored star each time he does a certain task. Then ten of those stars can be used to "purchase" a particular toy. Or twenty can be exchanged for some other item or service.

A token system has the double advantage of bestowing immediate and long-term benefits. The child receives some concrete reward (a star, chip, check mark, or whatever) each time he completes a task. At the same time, he can look forward to the possibility of turning in each of those intermediate tokens for a larger benefit at some time in the future. These tokens are often valuable in themselves to children, and they tend to become even more so as their trade-in value becomes apparent.

In Sandy's case, I thought that the tokens could be check marks, initialed by Mrs. Jones. They could be on a sheet attached to the refrigerator door, so that both could see them accumulate. In other words, every time Sandy got up on time, dressed on time, ate breakfast on time, and met the bus on time, she would be entitled to one or more check marks. This way, Sandy would have some small but concrete benefits as she got ready for school.

After a few minutes of serious calculation, Mrs. Jones decided that she could afford for Sandy to go at least once a week to the skating rink. Getting through her morning routine for five days would earn Sandy this reward. In other words, the necessary five check marks could be earned in a week of school days. But even if more than five school days were required, she would still eventually earn her reward. Mom would have to agree to let Sandy go within one week of the day she earned enough points.

Mrs. Jones felt sure this would work. So she sounded out Sandy casually about it one evening, and when the girl showed some interest, we decided to go ahead. But the questions remained whether Sandy would go along with the idea and change her behavior.

At the beginning of the next negotiating session, Mrs. Jones stated her offer: If Sandy would get up on time and be dressed and ready for the school bus when it came, she would get a point or check mark for that day. An agreed-upon number of points would then earn her a skating expedition.

Sandy looked up at her mother expectantly. For the first time, I thought I saw a spark of interest.

"What do you think?" the mother asked the girl.

"Would you really let me go?" Sandy responded. Sandy's mother had refused permission so many times in the past that Sandy was naturally suspicious. But she finally agreed.

I thought it was a good idea to put this agreement into writing, and I had suggested this possibility to the mother before we had begun the final negotiating session.

Mrs. Jones used my suggestion as an opportunity to explain the concept to her daughter. "This is as much for your protection as anything else, Sandy. I might forget part of what we've said—or you might forget, too. So if we put it all down in writing, we're sure to know exactly where we stand."

Sandy readily agreed. She even grew quite animated as the two of them started drawing up the contract. But she was concerned that she might not hear her mother some morning when she was called to get up. As a result, she feared she might be penalized unfairly. So they included a clause saying that Mrs. Jones had to be sure that her daughter heard her when she called. But she was to call at most only two times. You'll notice that this agreement required both Sandy *and* her mother to change their behavior in the morning.

As they drafted the contract, several other details came up that neither of them had considered during their oral discussion. One of the beauties of writing down a deal is that it makes you think more clearly and comprehensively.

With all the major concerns having been aired and put into

writing, the two of them drafted a final copy. Then they each signed the agreement. I've reproduced a copy of it below.

As you'll see, it's a little different from the mother's original plan because Sandy wanted to get points for carrying out each part of the morning's routine. (I also thought that this was a good idea.) In addition, because getting on the bus was the main requirement, this action got the most points.

MORNING ROUTINE

Sandy will get up within 5 minutes of being called, after either the first or second call. _____ 1 point

Sandy will dress and appear in the kitchen within 15 minutes after the first wake-up call, with, at the most, one further reminder. _____ 1 point

Sandy will finish breakfast within 30 minutes after the first call. _____ 1 point

Sandy will be ready to go when the school bus stops outside. _____ 3 points

Sandy can go skating when she has twenty-five points—as soon as Mother can arrange it.

[Signed]

Sandy: _____

Mom: _____

POINT CHART

M T W Th F M T W Th F M T W Th F

Up (1)
Dressed (1)
Breakfast (1)
Bus (3)

As I left them, this parent and child were communicating with each other again, and the youngster was learning many things about the business of life that would help her as she got ready to face the demands of the adult world.

This negotiating encounter demonstrates clearly that written contracts and token systems often go hand-in-hand. But more needs to be said about the details of instituting an effective token system in homes with children of different ages and varying negotiating skills.

We've already discussed how the fact of giving rewards to children for good behavior can seem somehow undesirable, like bribery. When misunderstood, the token system may appear to be an insidious kind of "payoff." That misconception can cause some parents to question this approach—and miss out on one of the most effective means for resolving difficult issues with their children.

To get the whole subject in perspective, think back on how you received gold stars in school for doing good work. Do you remember how great those little stickers made you feel? Such rewards are nothing more than tokens! When they're used properly, tokens can be an extremely effective means of promoting good behavior and positive habits.

There are many, many variations on the gold-star theme. I know of one teacher who gives her class a gold star every time all the pupils in the class complete their homework. When the entire class has earned a prearranged number of stars, she stages a pizza party or ice cream party for the whole group. I'm sure she gets as much enjoyment from the children's pleasure as they get from their reward.

"It's a lot easier than thinking up punishments for the kids who don't do their homework," the teacher says. "And this approach tends to encourage the class to pull together as a team." She explains that her gold-star system makes the youngsters in her care "feel special." There's no doubt that a youngster who feels good about himself and is used to getting positive strokes for good behavior is going to be more productive and much easier to work with.

Are there any dangers to the token system? Suppose children always got tokens for their good behavior and never got the positive, affectionate interactions that we think should always accompany them. In that case, they might develop a cold and mercenary attitude about their relations with other people. But that result should never come to pass with negotiated arrangements that are conducted in a spirit of love.

As you can see from the examples we've considered, there are many variations on the token system concept. Whatever the variation, here are some things to keep in mind.

• *Keep everything visible.* For very young children especially, the tokens that have been earned should be easy to see. To this end, you could make a chart similar to a calendar. Every time your child performs a given task, you could paste a star or sticker on the chart—or just sign your initials.

The number of tokens necessary for any available reward should be displayed clearly, in a way the child can understand. This is especially important with children who are not thoroughly familiar with numerical concepts. It's also important to award the token when the child is there to see you do it; and when the child is presented with the award, the parents should be sure to show their appreciation to him.

In other words, if your child puts all her toys away, she gets a clearly visible sticker as her reward. Then, after she gets five stars, she might be entitled to a more valuable reward, such as a small gift, a trip to the zoo, or going out for Saturday lunch. It can be helpful to put a picture of the bigger treat on the chart as an incentive—along with a clear indication of how much the treat will cost. You could put a photograph of the zoo, a toy, or something else on the space where the last star is to be placed. Finally, if you use stars or stickers and you provide a choice of rewards, be sure to make it easy for the child to change his mind along the way about which reward he wants to work for.

• *Make your tokens immediate.* An important principle to remember, especially in dealing with very young children, is that the goals must be kept very short term. Some older children will also want more immediate rewards; they may not want to wait even a day or two for their benefits.

One mother I know keeps a grab bag of little toys from the local variety store on hand. Whenever her five-year-old son straightens up his room and puts all his toys away neatly, he gets to pull something out of the grab bag. The suspense, along with the prospect of getting an attractive toy, adds a bit of excitement to the token concept.

Once the child has accumulated five of these little figures, which only cost a few pennies each, he is entitled to some special treat on the weekend—usually a more expensive toy or perhaps some ice cream from the local shop.

In this case, each of the cheap little toys has become a token. But at the same time, each token has value in itself in addition to its trade-in value after a given number of tokens have been accumulated.

• *Keep the system clear and simple.* Very young children can easily get confused when you add complexities to the system, such as bonuses or different types of tokens for different rewards. They may have trouble remembering which tokens lead to various rewards or what combinations they must earn to get a particular toy or treat.

Complex systems can backfire because children need to know exactly where they stand when they're earning their tokens. If the system you set up would strain even an adult's comprehension or patience, then it's certainly going to be overwhelming for a child. So keep it simple!

• *Use objective criteria for token awards.* A token system is too complicated when it demands difficult judgments about subjective behavior. For example, even a very young child can see when all his toys are put away. He's also aware when all the food on his plate has been eaten. In these cases, he can readily understand when he's entitled to a token and when he's not.

But it is difficult for him to judge more nebulous notions, such as what constitutes "good" behavior in a given situation. In other words, you don't want to make the reward of a token dependent upon whether he's been a "good boy" or even upon whether he's "behaved himself." Instead, being good or behaving properly must be defined in very specific terms.

Suppose, for example, that you've been having trouble with your four-year-old child acting up when you go shopping at the supermarket. He touches things when he's not supposed to, wanders away from you, runs up and down the aisles, and pushes the shopping cart too fast whenever he gets his hands on it.

Finally you decide to enter into negotiations to get him to stop doing these things. In your mind, all these actions may constitute "bad behavior." But for him, they have to be spelled out—*explicitly.* So you tell him each of the things that's bothering you, and then you make him an offer. If he avoids certain offensive actions—which you *list* for him— he'll receive one or more tokens, which he can exchange for something. (Perhaps the tokens can be money that he can use to buy some treat.) But if he does any of the forbidden things, he won't get as many—or any—tokens.

Obviously, with a true negotiation, your child will have to agree to the terms. If he does agree—and if the terms are clear—you'll have a much more effective way of monitoring his behavior than if you just require him to "be good."

• *Be consistent in keeping your agreements.* What if your child wins a reward, but also has done something that you haven't included in your list—even though it's clearly bad behavior? Should he still receive his reward?

In my opinion, if the youngster has observed all the conditions you've listed in an agreement, he should receive the token. You can always put any new offenses on your list in your next negotiation. But when you're in the midst of working out a deal in practice, it's important to maintain your credibility with your child. If you change the rules in midstream, it's likely that he'll become suspicious of you and your ability to negotiate will be impaired.

• *Write down the terms of your token system.* If your child cannot yet read, it may seem foolish to write the terms of the contract. But remember: A contract is intended to help *you* remember as much as your youngster.

You can also use a written contract at this stage as a learning tool. If you keep the terms of the contract and the token system simple, you can print them in easy-to-understand language and go over them in detail with your child. Among other things, you can teach him the meaning of each of the words that you've used—and thereby help him with his vocabulary and reading.

By recording the terms of the agreement, you're helping your child establish good habits for the future. Among other things, you'll be encouraging him to think clearly and precisely in formulating the final terms of the agreement. To this end, you may want your youngster to write down one or more of the terms of the arrangement himself.

Here are some additional considerations to keep in mind when you set up a token system for more mature youngsters:

• *Delayed gratification will work better with older children.* A child's concept of time becomes more sophisticated with age. Still it doesn't always work to say: "If you'll do such-and-such, I give you a special reward next month."

In other words, even with an older child, promising a new bicycle or a big trip next year may not have much appeal. But if you set up a token system, the child can see step-by-step progress and is more likely to work consistently toward his goal.

In general, I think seven or eight is a good age to begin introducing longer periods of delayed gratification into a token system.

• *Older children can use more sophisticated token systems.* Generally speaking, stars and stickers are not going to work as well with older children as with younger ones. A good substitute token that's used by a number of people I know is poker chips. When a child accumulates a specified number, he can cash them in for whatever prize he's been working toward. On the other hand, poker chips can be lost quite easily, so they aren't always suitable, and their rather easy availability may tempt your child to cheat.

With teenagers, you can get even more sophisticated. A counting system or checklist will generally work for them. Young teens and older preteens often like to use real bankbooks. Or you might buy a spiral notebook and list at the top of each page agreed-upon chores for the teenager and the payment for each.

Mowing the lawn might entitle your teenager to five checks; doing the dishes might be worth two; and taking out the garbage might rate one check. He could pool his various checks and exchange them for rewards. For example, he might "buy" one use of the family car for five checks, or perhaps a one-dollar increase in his week's allowance for four checks.

• *Watch out for failure clauses.* For older children, especially, you may want to ask for higher performance and give points or rewards less frequently. But when you do, don't build in a feature that permits your child to fail and lose many points or much effort. Even worse, don't set him up to fail halfway through a task and thus destroy his incentive to continue with the deal. For example, suppose you arrange to give your child use of the car each weekend if he gets points for finishing his homework *every* night before a school day. Here a failure clause has been built into the contract: If your child doesn't finish his work on Tuesday, let's say, there will be no advantage for him to finish it on Wednesday or Thursday. You'll be embarrassed if your child figures this out before you do! In such a case, it would have been better to give independent points for each day's achievement and then let those points carry over to the next week.

• *Don't tempt your child to cheat.* Successful cheating is not a good experience for a child, nor is catching a cheater a helpful experience for a parent. It's always better to be in a position to reward honesty than to punish fraud. Best of all is to arrange things so there will be little temptation to cheat because it will be too difficult.

In an effort to encourage honesty, parents who use check marks for tokens might initial each mark. And if you use poker chips, be sure your child isn't getting some from a "contraband" source! If you have more than one child, you might want to check periodically to be sure one isn't coercing another to get his chips.

These are some of the considerations that you should keep in mind if you're thinking about incorporating a token system into your negotiations with your children. But with tokens, as with written contracts in general, it's important to keep a couple of caveats in mind.

First of all, if you're using tokens, always remember to be

positive. That means do not fall into the trap of building punishments into your system.

One mother I know was concerned about the constant fighting that occurred between her son and daughter. Every day when they came home from school, they would argue instead of playing together peacefully. To remedy the problem, the mother decided to try a token system. Whenever the children played together without arguing before supper, she said she would give each one a token. The children, in turn, could accumulate the tokens and cash them in later for some reward.

Unfortunately she went one step too far—and ended up ruining the entire system. Her mistake? The mother pressed hard to have the right to *take tokens back* whenever the children quarreled.

This seemed to work for a short time. But the day finally arrived when the children had no tokens to give back! In fact they were in the hole. The reason? For several days they had been quarreling more often than they had been peaceful.

In effect the children moved into a "minus token" situation, and they were faced with having to climb out of a hole so that they could begin to accumulate tokens and move once more toward their rewards. This lack of incentive killed the agreement. It almost always does. The children lose interest, and the token system falls apart.

This arrangement would have worked if the mother had simply emphasized the positive aspect of their agreement. On a day when an argument occurred, she could have withheld giving a token—but at the same time, it would have been better *not* to have subtracted one. In this way the children would have been encouraged to continue striving toward their goals, even if they missed a day of earning a token.

Here again, we have another example of why it's so important to emphasize the positive instead of the negative in negotiating sessions with your youngsters.

Finally let me offer another word about written contracts. If certain family members enjoy writing out the "deals" that are arrived at, then that may well be the best system for them. On the other hand, some families prefer to stick with verbal agreements, sealed with a handshake, because they feel that this approach reflects more of a trust of family members in each other.

Obviously there's no single right or wrong way to set up a system of rewards or close a negotiating session. The main thing is just to be aware of the options. Then you'll be in a better position to choose an approach that will keep all parties feeling secure and satisfied.

6.

Back to the Bargaining Table

*Y*OU'VE worked hard to hammer out an agreement. You've spent time in thought and discussion, working out an arrangement that both you and your child accept. Perhaps you've even gone to the trouble of committing the agreement to paper. For a while everyone keeps to the agreement.

Then things begin to go haywire.

Your child falls back into his old negative habits and patterns. The rewards he originally agreed to don't seem to appeal anymore. He doesn't respond when you make some gentle suggestions that maybe he should live up to his commitments and respect his relationship with his parents a little more.

You also notice that you're slipping back into old patterns. You're beginning to complain and sermonize.

Something just isn't right. So what do you do?

You don't scream. You don't head for the woodshed. You don't lash out in any way. Instead, you return to the bargaining table.

In the outside world, bargains break down all the time as

conditions change and require new solutions. Governments violate the terms of treaties. Labor or management fails to live up to expectations. Divorced spouses violate marital settlements.

If this happens so often outside the home, it's natural to assume that it will happen inside the home as well. After all, neither children nor adults are perfect. They're going to make mistakes, and they're going to allow their short-range self-interest to get out of control at times. If the result is that your agreement doesn't seem to be doing the job—if the problem your agreement was intended to solve is still with you—then the main idea is not to explode. Instead, get your relationship back on the right track with some intelligent renegotiation.

Renegotiation is the lubricating force that keeps the initial process of negotiation working, without your having to resort to quick-fix measures like punishment. To determine whether renegotiation is in order, there are several points you should consider. I like to think in terms of several "renegotiation questions."

Question 1. Are you getting enough out of your agreement?

Both your child *and* you must profit from negotiations. Negotiated agreements, as we've seen in our examples, may be of two types. In order to determine the type of renegotiation that may be called for, it's important to distinguish between the two.

In the first type, the parents feel it's essential for their child to do or not do something. It's also important that there be few or no lapses in his behavior. One example would be heedlessly bicycling across a busy street. Some important moral issues fall into this class.

In the second type, the parents' aim is less extreme—it's just to increase good behavior or decrease the seriousness of a problem. Getting your child to do more homework or be more helpful around the house are illustrations.

The agreement in the first case is more in the nature of a binding contract. Both parties agree that they definitely will perform as promised. In the second case, the agreement is more an arrangement to exchange services. In other words, the idea is "If you help us, we will help you." If afterward the child finds that the services he is offered are insufficient, the agreement may not be fully followed. Most token systems are of this second type.

It's important for a number of reasons not to confuse these types of agreements. In the first, if a failure occurs, an immediate renegotiation may be necessary. Or if the problem is dangerous or serious enough, some other form of decisive intervention may be required.

In the second, the more common situation, parents should be careful not to overreact to a failure. The situation is probably not dangerous or crucial in some way to the child's development—and you also may be getting a lot more out of the youngster than you did before. For example, a child's room that was *never* presentable may now be fairly clean—if not regularly, at least usually. Some mornings, perhaps your child just doesn't have enough time to clean his room and at the same time meet all his daily appointments. On other days, however, he has learned to be diligent enough to please any reasonable parent.

In this second type of agreement, you may come to feel

that you're offering too much for what you're getting and therefore renegotiations may be in order. Perhaps the child has been able to become "wealthy" without really complying with some of your most important aims. The possibility of renegotiating operates as a safety valve to keep you from overreacting here. In other words, you shouldn't accuse your child of trying to weasel out of the obligations you thought you had imposed on him. Instead approach him calmly, explain your concerns, and reopen the discussions.

Reopening negotiations should not be considered a violation of the original agreement. In fact, it's helpful to include an explicit option to renegotiate after a given time as part of your original agreement. That way you can have a formal tool to monitor the agreement and be certain that both parties are getting sufficient benefits.

Question 2. Do you find yourself constantly nagging or coaxing your child to keep the agreement?

With very young children, an occasional reminder about the terms of your agreement is quite appropriate. Suppose you have struck a bargain that provides Johnny will get ready for bed willingly in return for a token. So you say, "It's time for bed. Let me see you smile and hop to it so I can give you a sticker."

Such reminders for young children are perfectly acceptable. They may have been provided for in the agreement itself. But coaxing and nagging are not. In general the difference between a reminder and nagging is both in the number of times you have to say something and in the way you say it. When you find yourself reminding your child about the cost of failing to meet his agreements with you, or repeating, "Don't forget to pick up your toys," over and over again, that's nagging. You're adding a negative factor to the situation that the agreement was designed to avoid.

Coaxing, on the other hand, may at first seem more acceptable. Your voice does not have the negative, harsh quality, and your tone and manner may be pleasant and agreeable. But if you find yourself cajoling or pleading for your child to keep his bargain, that's a dead giveaway. You've moved beyond the realm of acceptable reminders.

The problem with nagging and coaxing is that they defeat a major benefit of negotiating, which is the encouragement or self-discipline in your child. Your child should be developing his own ability to foresee the longer-term results of his actions. Instead the child may begin to use your pressure tactics as his reference point for proper action, rather than develop his own guides for his behavior.

The use of negative tactics will generate resentment and may very well become coercive. We all hate to be nagged, but it often works: We'll give in just to get the other person to keep quiet! But there may be unexpected repercussions. Parents who nag may encourage their children to use the same negative tactic against their elders! The adults may thus heap hot coals on their own heads!

In any event, if you find that you've become involved in regular coaxing or nagging, that's a sign that the bargain may be breaking down. It may be time to go back to the table and try to sort through what's wrong and how you can get back on track in your relationship with your child. Perhaps you need another set of rewards to motivate him. Or you may simply have to rethink your approach to following up on a negotiated deal and step back out of the trap.

Question 3. Do you find yourself getting angry or resorting to threats to get your child to go along with the agreement?

A negotiated settlement is supposed to keep the peace in the family. But often—especially for those who are not accustomed to dealing positively with their children—it's easy to get frustrated. It's also easy to resort to the heavy hand in an attempt to *force* the agreement to work.

I'm reminded of one father who put together what he thought was a beautifully constructed system of rewards to encourage his overweight twelve-year-old son to do calisthenics on a regular basis. This was part of a program to decrease calorie intake and increase exercise. The father was willing to monitor the program, but when he and his son began to try to put their agreement into effect the father tended to get impatient. The son would usually begin quite well, with some push-ups and perhaps some sit-ups. But then he'd get bored or distracted and would do everything he could to avoid doing his toe-touches or other stretching exercises.

The father began with gentle nagging: "If you don't finish up these exercises, you're not going to get any reward!" Day by day he heard himself sliding gradually into a more forceful tone of voice and issuing extra-agreement threats: "If I have to keep yelling at you to get these exercises done, I'll see that you don't eat anything but bean sprouts and liver for dinner!"

Such an approach destroys the benefits of a negotiated settlement. It moves the parent and child back into the old coercive situation—and punishment gets substituted for positive motivation.

The right approach here, as the father finally learned, was

simply to *remind* the boy one or maybe two times in a calm, low-key manner, "You know, you have to finish all your exercises in order to get your reward."

If the boy failed to respond, he didn't get the benefit promised by the original agreement. It was as simple as that. No threats. No anger. Just calm, decisive action in accordance with the agreement. If that isn't enough, as happened in this particular case, it will be necessary to renegotiate the deal.

In this case the father realized that *some* rewards should be made available to the boy if he did a certain percentage of his exercises. He had made the mistake of making any reward dependent on doing all the scheduled exercises. As a result, if the boy saw he wasn't going to finish all the exercises, he would also see he'd get no reward. So he would quit halfway through and refuse to continue. The child was just being logical!

So they made a new agreement. The boy still wouldn't get the full benefits of a complete calisthenics session unless he went through the entire routine. But if he did part of the exercises, he would get a partial reward. The father also cleverly arranged for the reward for the last half of the schedule to be greater than for the first half. He realized that the second half would be more stressful for the boy, as well as more beneficial. In this way, without an all-or-nothing approach, the boy would always have an incentive to pursue at least part of the exercise regimen. And the more he did the more he could earn.

If you find yourself falling back on threats or getting angry because the negotiated agreement is not working out as you expected, it may be that you simply need to "back off." First calmly see if the withholding of benefits—without threats—will cause your child to behave as he agreed. If this doesn't work, you'll need to go back to the bargaining table.

Question 4. Why has the contract failed?

If it's clear that the deal you've made with your child has fallen apart, you should try to identify precisely why. The first thing to look at is whether the reward system needs revising. Here are some possibilities:

• You may find the rewards you originally arranged have become boring. They are no longer so rewarding. Perhaps you've agreed to buy your son baseball cards every time he performs certain acceptable behavior. But after a while, almost any youngster is going to outgrow or get tired of baseball cards, and the contract has provided no alternative.

• Many parents also find that a contract is not working because they have placed their rewards too far in the future. Or if a token system is being used, the points themselves may be awarded too long after they have been earned. Remember that fundamental truth of negotiating with children: You shouldn't delay gratification too far into the future. If you do, your deal will lack the proper incentives for your child to perform up to par.

• Your child may not be able to follow the way the rewards work. For example, he may not know how many points he has or how many he needs. You may not have made that information readily available, or your arrangement may be so complicated he can't figure it out.

• You may have failed to come through with a promised reward. Or, you may have been delivering it even when the child didn't carry through his end. Don't yield to pleas: "But Mom, I *tried,* but I just couldn't." Such tender-heartedness will doom your agreement!

• Adult affection may be missing or too perfunctory.

• The rewards may be set up on an all-or-nothing basis. In

other words, if the child completes part of a requirement but not the whole thing, he won't receive any benefit.

• The rewards may "cost" too much—i.e., they may require the child to perform too many duties.

• The rewards may be too cheap—and the child is satisfied too easily.

Note that I haven't listed here, as a reason for the breakdown of an agreement, that your child has become demanding, devious, or stubborn. To reach such conclusions is to blame your child instead of your agreement. That will soon lead you back into the nasty game of mutual accusations, anger, and hostility.

In any case, it's important to track down the precise reasons why the contract has fallen apart. Otherwise you'll lack sufficient knowledge to proceed with effective renegotiations.

Now let's assume you've asked and answered these initial questions about renegotiation, and you determine that you want to restructure your deal. What strategies should you follow as you begin the process of renegotiation?

STRATEGIES FOR RENEGOTIATION

You're back at the bargaining table. You know there was a breakdown somewhere in the original agreement, and you have to correct the problem.

Your child will undoubtedly have a dozen or more creative ideas about how to correct the situation. You know the typical responses:

• "I'm willing to give up vegetables, but I promise to eat all my dessert."

• "I'm willing to sacrifice a few hours of sleep if we can just set my curfew a little later."

You can imagine any number of other such proposals. But

115

as a responsible parent, you'll find you need to come into this second wave of negotiations, as you did in the first, with your own "menu" of bargaining options.

The original rules for negotiating, by the way, are still in effect. They must be followed just as you followed them before. In the time that has passed since you struck your first deal, you haven't become a doormat to be walked over by sharp, persuasive offspring. At the same time, the youngsters aren't marine recruits ready to be bossed around by a parental drill sergeant.

We've discussed several things to keep in mind as you attempt to troubleshoot for weaknesses in your original agreement. Now let's look more closely at some of the most important of these rules.

Rule 1. Shorten the interval between the child's performance and the tokens or rewards.

Undoubtedly you considered the issue of delayed gratification during your initial negotiations. You probably structured the deal in a way that you felt would give your youngster sufficiently short-term rewards. But you may have been wrong.

Your child's perception of time is almost certainly quite different from your own, especially if he is very young. A minute becomes an hour to a five-year-old; an hour can seem like a week; and a week can be forever. This limited understanding of time reduces the willingness of very young children to wait for rewards. It may be that you've miscalculated the maturity of your youngster's concept of time.

Even older children may lack the means of dealing with relatively long time periods. Ellen, a nine-year-old third-grade student, wasn't doing very well in school. Her teacher assured her concerned parents that she had the basic ability, but she seemed to lack the motivation. She wasted classroom study time and often ended up hurrying to complete her work at the last minute. As a result Ellen made many careless mistakes, especially in arithmetic. Ellen's parents had frequently and forcefully explained how important arithmetic was for her future, and how concerned they were. But Ellen's apparent distaste for this subject was too great, or so it seemed, since these pleas and explanations hadn't helped.

After consultations with the teacher, Ellen's parents negotiated a deal with Ellen whereby the girl would receive a new bicycle if she brought home a sufficiently good report card at the end of the school year. Her marks didn't have to be straight As. They had agreed that at least one A and two Bs would be sufficient. These marks would reflect her ability and show some effort on her part.

At first Ellen was so delighted with the idea of earning a bicycle that her performance began to improve dramatically. But her progress was short-lived. Her grades began to decline once again until finally she was back at the level where she had started.

When her parents confronted her for the second time about her poor performance in her schoolwork, Ellen had no explanation. She knew she had given up soon after she had embarked on this new program, but she replied quite honestly, "I don't know why."

It became apparent that Ellen had somehow lost her initial enthusiasm for the new bicycle. It wasn't that she didn't care about the bike or didn't want it. She still spoke as if it was important to her. But the possibility of receiving the bike wasn't changing her study behavior, mainly because it was taking too long to earn the reward.

To sum up, the original agreement with Ellen had three

features that needed to be improved: (1) The parents had arranged for only a single reward—the bicycle. (2) They had made that reward depend on an entire year's good work. In conversations with Ellen, it became clear that the girl was very worried that she wouldn't make any As at all, and so much of her effort might be entirely lost. (3) The reward was very far in the future, and there weren't clear indications along the way as to whether she would be able to earn it.

The parents understood the main issues they had to grapple with in the renegotiation procedure. Together the parents and the child conceived a plan to give Ellen points for getting her schoolwork done every day. And when Ellen suggested it, they agreed to rent a bicycle each weekend to give Ellen a regular intermediate reward if she completed her schoolwork during the week in a satisfactory way. They also reduced the grade requirement, to a B— average.

This way, Ellen could enjoy learning to ride and keep her interest level high, even before she received the ultimate reward. She was able to sample the pleasure the bicycle would give her, even as she made progress collecting more and more points for satisfactory schoolwork.

At the same time, when she completed the school year on the original terms of the contract, she would be entitled to have her own new bike as a kind of "grand prize."

The new contract turned out to be quite effective. Ellen's study habits improved significantly as she worked hard each week to gain the right to ride the rental bike over the weekend. And she performed well enough over the long haul to qualify for her new bike at the end of the year.

In this case, the renegotiation strategy worked like a charm. The time intervals between the reward to be earned and the commendable behavior that earned the reward were short enough to keep the youngster's motivation high and her attention keen.

Rule 2. Give your child more of your own time and attention, in addition to the material rewards.

Sometimes a very attractive and expensive item may appear to be just the thing to get a child moving during initial negotiations. Both parent and child may agree wholeheartedly that this particular toy or trip is just what's required to change a child's behavior. In actual practice the reward may fall short because both parent and child have overlooked the importance of the human element in bestowing the reward.

One six-year-old child had agreed to practice the piano regularly in return for a series of gifts involving a rather expensive set of dolls, doll clothing, and doll furniture that had been advertised on television. The child earned "pieces" of the set by practicing each day, so that eventually she would be able to earn the entire set. But the youngster started losing interest. She practiced inconsistently, despite the seeming attractiveness of the rewards.

When the father and daughter sat down to rethink the deal they had worked out, an important factor came to light. It seems that the adult often took the girl's older brother fishing on weekends, but he spent very little time alone with the girl.

Picking up on this cue, the father couched his renegotiation strategy this way: He said he would sit and listen to her playing each day for the last five minutes of her twenty-minute practice—and he promised to be an interested and enthusiastic audience.

Whenever she had practiced for five days for the full time

without complaining, he would take her on a special "date." He promised that just the two of them would take a trip to McDonald's for a hamburger or perhaps to the local park for an outing.

The daughter immediately agreed, and the arrangement worked beautifully. The key was not just the more attractive material reward; a very real incentive for her was the added special attention from her daddy.

Another parent, a single mother, had to be breadwinner, nanny, housekeeper, laundress, cook, and gardener in the home. She found herself being pushed over the edge when her three- and four-year-old daughters refused to take their afternoon nap without an all-out battle.

The nap was important for several reasons. First of all, the youngsters needed the rest. If they didn't have an hour or so of sleep in the middle of each day, they turned into absolute terrors by dinnertime. And the mother, who did a great deal of work at home, needed a quiet period each day to conduct her business.

Because of the importance she placed on these naps, the mother tended to get panicky and even hysterical when her young daughters balked. Instead of dealing with them in a calm fashion, she resorted to begging, pleading, yelling, and physical punishment—with disastrous effect.

Then she decided to try to negotiate.

At first she promised her children a small reward if they rested quietly during naptime. She offered them small plastic toys, and this worked like a charm. They went right to sleep, with no arguments. But when the novelty began to wear off, so did the ceasefire.

The mother decided to *re*negotiate the bargain.

Her solution was to focus on the additional love and attention she could give the children, rather than a search for additional material rewards. The daughters didn't specifically ask for this change in the reward system, but the mother felt that sometimes they just wanted extra attention from her. When she suggested that she might find time for them to do other things together, they were quite pleased. From the point of view of the family's finances this new arrangement was good because there was very little extra cash available.

Specifically, this mother cut out several colorful cards in different shapes, and she drew a picture of a different activity or adventure on the back of each. Then she dumped all the cards into a small fishbowl, where the children could see them clearly.

Before each nap time, she let the children draw a card from the bowl and tuck it under their pillows. When they rested without a struggle, their cards could be exchanged immediately for the various activities that the mother had listed on them.

Each of those activities or outings, though they were all inexpensive, involved opportunities for the children to spend more enjoyable time with their mother. The activities included such things as reading their favorite book, five minutes of being pushed on the swings in the yard, making popcorn, and having a squirt-gun "war" with their mother on the front lawn.

Eventually, of course, the novelty of these "activity cards" began to wear off. But the basic concept remained workable. All the mother had to do was to create new cards, with new activities involving loving interaction between the mother and the children.

So whenever you're renegotiating a contract with your child, try to come up with rewards that involve stimulation, learning, or loving experiences. It's a basic principle of negotiating with children that what a youngster may want most is *you*. Financial or material incentives can help, especially as the children get older. But at any age, the human enhancements to a relationship are essential. If you take this approach, I think you'll discover in the long run that you've received as many rewards from negotiated settlements as has your child!

Of course this is not to say that you should only have loving interactions with your children as a result of a negotiation. But the power of love during negotiating sessions can certainly add to the harmony in your home and help your children develop into the adults you want them to be.

Rule 3. Beef up your rewards by eliminating "freebies."

As you know, the main objective of negotiating agreements with children is to change their behavior for the better. But if no negotiation seems to work in a given situation, then you may want to revise the way goods and services are delivered in your home.

Sometimes parents find even at the beginning of a negotiation that they have trouble thinking of rewards to offer their children. Perhaps they have been generous and have already given their children whatever they could. Now the children are getting an overabundance of "freebies." In such a case, parents may want to take back some free privileges and services they've already bestowed and use them as rewards.

Sometimes, but perhaps less often than you'd think, this can cause your children to become quite unhappy. Benefits that have become part of the family routine present the greatest resistance to change. These often include allowances and other weekly or daily privileges or services. In contrast, one-of-a-kind or infrequent benefits usually lend themselves more easily to negotiation.

It's amazing how easy it often is to take back benefits, even routine ones, when contracts are negotiated calmly. Many times children are pleased just to be included in a negotiation, and they'll willingly agree that there is indeed a problem with the lack of rewards that needs to be solved. The idea of earning something, even something that has previously been free, can give them a sense of accomplishment that is rewarding in itself.

One such case involved eight-year-old Susie, who had agreed to set the table for the evening meal as an addition to her weekly allowance. But after a few days she usually refused to do it, and when she did, it was only with much fussing and complaining.

So her mother, who was savvy in the subtleties of negotiation, decided that the extra money Susie made from table-setting was much too little to motivate her. Mom had noticed that whenever Susie said she wanted anything, she or her husband were all too willing to buy it for her.

As the mother began to search for an appropriate freebie to take back, the allowance seemed a good place to begin. But the mother rejected the idea, even though setting the table was directly tied to that allowance. Why? It was clear that Susie didn't need or particularly care for the money.

Instead the mother looked for another, more valuable reward that would be related directly to the consequences of the broken bargain. As she searched for a solution, it occurred to her that Susie's failure to help get the meal on the table on time tended to squeeze all the family's activities later in the evening. Susie's television viewing was jeopardized by the delays.

So the mother reopened negotiations like this: "Susie,

when you don't keep your bargain to help me get supper on the table at a reasonable hour, that means we get finished eating later. So you get started on your homework later, and you have less time to do the things that you want to do.

"Up to now, I've been rather liberal about letting you stay up a little late to watch television. But now it seems to me you'll have to make time earlier for watching TV. Otherwise, it's only right that you should miss out."

The mother is presenting the question in a way that implies she wants to reopen the negotiation. She doesn't present it as a demand. This move is sure to get Susie's attention. The mother has put Susie into a "down" position and given her something to bargain for. In doing this, though, it's essential to avoid presenting the take-back as a punishment. Otherwise, Susie will be likely to try for some form of retaliation or resistance.

After the renegotiation, the same terms of the original agreement remained, with Susie getting part of her weekly allowance in return for helping with the evening meal. But in addition to losing that part of her allowance if she failed to comply, she would *also* fail to get a part of her television viewing because of the delay that she had created in getting the family meal ready.

In other words, in the renegotiation the mother put a price on the girl's failure to comply. Putting the arrangement this way made it look "natural," and not as though it were simply a punishment. As a result, Susie agreed to the proposal.

This mother was wise to use the loss of TV time as a direct consequence of the broken bargain. The deprivation is easier to see than if she had chosen to take back some other privilege. Of course it isn't essential to do it this way. But if you settle on a less direct approach, be careful! When the relationship between a lost freebie and the desired behavior isn't clear, the bargain is more likely to break down.

For example, suppose you tell Susie that if she doesn't help with the table setting, her friend Janey can't come to play with her the next day. That consequence has no direct bearing on your problem. You are in effect suspending a privilege that was already granted and that is unrelated to the consequences of the broken bargain. It's more difficult to arrange this so that your child won't respond to it as if it were a punishment.

Of course, each child and each situation have to be treated individually. Susie might not have cared much about having her allowance docked. But Bob was quite different. He had negotiated for an addition to his allowance of five dollars a week in return for his agreement to help out around the home. But the help wasn't specified clearly. Bob, like many teenagers, needed that money to help support his social life.

After agreeing to these basic terms, however, Bob began to neglect a couple of his regular household duties—taking out the garbage and mowing the lawn. His allowance had been continued and so in effect had become a freebie because he was doing little to earn it. The parents had broken the agreement by paying the allowance without requiring anything in return. Finally, his father reopened negotiations by taking a second look at Bob's allowance. He explained again that he felt Bob was old enough to accept greater responsibilities for the allowance he got. By now the boy was old enough not to expect so much unearned generosity from his parents. After all, he couldn't expect an unlimited supply of freebies from other people!

This argument made the arrangement for the allowance

seem more reasonable to Bob—though he certainly didn't say he liked it!

Specifically, the father designated two dollars of Bob's allowance for the boy's garbage duty and three dollars for mowing the lawn. If Bob failed to mow the lawn, he would definitely not be entitled to the three dollars for that week. By the same token, if he didn't take out the garbage, he would get his allowance minus two dollars.

After serious discussions, which sometimes grew heated, the two agreed on a modification. The father found some other tasks that Bob could do to recoup his lost allowance, just in case he neglected to mow the lawn and take out the garbage.

By using this approach, the father didn't resort to suspending the boy's allowance—which is a popular punishment used by many parents. Instead he made the full allowance dependent upon the teenager's more conscientious commitment to work around the home. The consequences of his not receiving a full allowance were clearly related to his failure to do the designated chores.

The technique of taking back freebies, then, can be a subtle and sometimes complex concept. It's not always easy to distinguish between reducing the freebies and meting out punishment.

To keep the distinction straight, the main principle to keep in mind is this: If you find yourself resorting to deprivations that are unrelated to the conduct you're trying to correct, then you're in danger of delivering punishment, and facing the child's retaliations that may result.

The best arrangement involves withholding benefits or privileges that are a direct and natural consequence of the correct behavior that you're trying to achieve. This is much easier to arrange in a way that won't appear to your child to be a punishment.

Rule 4. Be ready to engage in some extended—but civilized—verbal sparring with your child.

The process of renegotiation may not involve a simple, one-shot discussion between you and your child. Instead the discussions and interactions may take place in short exchanges over a period of days, as you go back and forth, trying to hammer out the final terms of a mutually acceptable arrangement. In any case, the parent must not just dictate the terms of the agreement.

Remember: You're dealing with at least two sets of volatile factors whenever a bargain breaks down:

1) Emotions often run high in any family confrontation—and the interpersonal aftermath of a broken contract is no exception.

2) The breakdown in the initial agreement indicates that the original problem may be more serious than you had supposed—and it will require more finesse to bring things to a final solution.

It's essential not to assume that everything is going to be wrapped up in one nice, neat renegotiation package. Consider what happened when an eleven-year-old boy, Larry, was having problems with his neighbor Frank. The two boys often got into loud arguments, and Larry's mother tried to resolve the situation by negotiating a bargain with the two boys together.

Specifically, the mother and both youngsters had agreed that she would supply the boys with regular snacks after play if they could just get along peacefully. But the arrangement never got off the ground.

A major problem was that Larry and Frank were not really compatible. They happened to be the only eleven-year-old boys in the neighborhood, and so naturally they sought one another's company, regardless of the potential problems. But there were many strains. They hardly even wanted to play the same games. Most of the time they started off with mild quarreling, regressed to yelling and insulting remarks, and ultimately ended up punching one another.

Larry's mother found herself playing referee. When there were repeated confrontations in the same day, she had the unpleasant task of sending Frank home—despite the fact that they were all supposed to be operating under a nego-tiated settlement designed to produce peace in play.

The mother realized she had very little leverage with Frank. Sending him home didn't seem to help, and Frank's parents weren't cooperative. Any renegotiation would have to focus on her own son, Larry. When she reopened negotia-tions with Larry alone, she quickly found that she was in for some difficult give-and-take.

"I don't think you and Frank should play together quite so often because you don't seem to get along very well," was the mother's opening gambit.

But Larry reacted with a typical tactic in strained negotiat-ing sessions—*the countercharge.*

"You're the one who's causing the problem—you're always yelling at us!" he said. An unfair charge, in this case, to be sure. But Larry was just lashing out. He seemed to get angry at the idea of even discussing the matter, and his response was designed to put his mother on the defensive and cut off the conversation.

Some parents might have responded in kind, and that would have been the end of any possibility for constructive discussion. But Larry's mother was smarter than that: "I don't enjoy yelling at you," she replied, not really responding directly to her son's charge. "So I think we should try real hard to find a solution to this fighting."

Here the mother used a negotiating maneuver that might be called *ignore and divert.* In other words, she didn't try to defend herself against an unjust charge, nor did she counterattack with a charge of her own. Instead, she ignored Larry's challenge to butt heads with her and immediately diverted his attention back to the real issue: changing Larry's behavior.

Larry quickly realized that he wasn't going to shut off the discussion with countercharges. But he wasn't in the mood for further negotiations, so he replied, "I don't want to talk about it."

The mother knew that pushing him at this point would only fan the flames of his anger. So she let the issue drop for the moment and finished her dinner preparations.

After the meal was over, she came back to the issue again. In effect she reopened the bargaining session with another positive comment. She said she felt it would definitely be possible for them to find a workable solution to the problem between Larry and Frank.

But Larry was still not in the mood to deal with his mother directly. He used a different technique to evade the issue this time—one that might be called *the sidestep.*

"If you'd leave us alone, we could work it out between us," Larry said. In other words, his solution to the problem was simply to let them have it out, with no intervention.

But his mother didn't fall for this, even though she recognized it was partly true. She was canny enough to realize that part of the boy's quarreling was just intended to get her to step in as a mediator. But they fought far too often even when she was nowhere near, and their quarrels had become too noisy to ignore. The mother wasn't about to let the neighbors settle the problem by calling the police. She decided to try a variation on the theme of reducing freebies, which we discussed in the previous section. She decided that Larry would be better off spending his time with other friends and activities, and so she looked around for a way to bring this about through a new negotiation.

She told Larry that since his relationship with Frank hadn't improved, she would have to separate them. In effect mother took back a freebie—the time she had been permitting the boys to play together. Larry would simply have to find other things to do with his free time. This was an extreme solution, certainly, and perhaps not the best one. In any case, this mother realized she would have to work hard to make it succeed.

In order to make this tactic workable, the mother realized that she would have to help Larry find some attractive alternative for the relationship with Frank. Larry was a retiring and generally not very assertive child. If she didn't help out, the suspension of the play privileges would be a serious deprivation, and it might be some time before Larry found other activities on his own.

This mother felt there were many activities that might be substituted for the unruly relationship that prevailed between the two boys.

When Larry's mother first told him she thought they should be separated, Larry balked. He didn't like the idea that he was being forced to stop this play relationship. After all, it was the only one he had!

Then his mother began to sweeten her offer: "I think swimming would be an especially good possibility for you," she said. "You would meet some new friends. And that would also mean you could go canoeing with the other boys when we go camping this summer." Interested silence.

"I've met the swimming instructor at the local Y, and he's really interested in talking to you," the mother continued. "He said that if you do well, he may be able to get you into a life-saving class in a year or so. That would prepare you to be a lifeguard."

Now Larry was *really* interested. He had always liked swimming. Suddenly, the stormy relationship with Frank seemed much less inviting.

Larry decided to go along with the negotiation. He agreed to stop playing with Frank entirely, and in return he got his mother's support to take the swimming lessons at the Y. Soon he was progressing very quickly. He found new friends and new activities. His hotheaded, highly physical behavior was channeled constructively through the negotiating process. Today, a few years later, he's a lifeguard at a camp during the summer, helping to pay his way through college.

If Larry's mother had been less tactful in pushing for a successful renegotiation, the consequences could have been serious. But she stuck with it, completed an arduous process involving numerous tough verbal exchanges, and both she and her son were happier and more satisfied as a result.

Sometimes no matter how often you go back to the bargaining table, you can't seem to work out a deal. Or you may reach a settlement, but your child openly and egregiously violates it. What should you do? There are several possible courses of action, some good and some bad, that you can take when bargaining breaks down.

7.

When Bargaining Breaks Down

*T*HE unsuccessful negotiation—it's inevitable. If it weren't, you wouldn't need to read this book!

Of course we can always hope that a settlement, reached after thoughtful, sensitive discussions, will stick. But the fact remains that between parents and offspring, bargains are struck and bargains are struck down.

What can you do when your hard-earned deal falls apart?

Let's say that the negotiating process has taken place, and an agreement was reached. The terms were thoroughly understood by both parties, and the deal was signed on the dotted line or sealed with a handshake.

You settle in for some relative calm and smooth sailing in your home. But then your daughter repeatedly breaks her promise to go to bed without a struggle . . . or your son flatly refuses to pick up his toys as agreed. You renegotiate again and again, but renegotiation fails every time.

You don't know what you can do. You have quarreled again with your children and with your spouse. Everyone feels guilty, and angry, and confused. You can give in and let your child's behavior go unchecked. Or you can look for someone to blame—your child, yourself, your spouse, the neighborhood children, or the evil world.

If you're a normal parent, you're apt to feel your blood begin a slow boil. An impulse that has been held back throughout the negotiation process may emerge strongly now. And that is—to *punish*. Deprive, spank, criticize, sermonize! Chances are good that if your feelings go unchecked, that's exactly what you'll do.

The impulse to punish is a deeply ingrained, natural reaction. So it's easy to rationalize. You can almost hear an insistent inner voice saying, "I gave my child a reasonable chance! I was fair and patient and cooperative! I lived up to my end of the bargain! I tried, I suffered, and now I've had enough."

You try patting yourself on the back. In your own eyes you've proven yourself the consummately broad-minded, evenhanded adult. After all, it was *your* idea to negotiate, wasn't it? How many other parents would have just lowered the boom in the first place?

But we're not concerned here about what other people might have done. Let's just talk about *you* and *your* child. Assume you have been fair and equitable in the negotiating process. But something went wrong. You've run out of negotiating ideas. Now you're confronted with the need to do some damage control.

What are your options? First of all, don't give in to the high emotions of the moment. You certainly want to avoid unpleasant scenes. A series of explosions between parent and child may have a wonderful effect, in the short run, but this is hardly in the spirit of responsible child-rearing—which is the ultimate goal of the negotiating process.

It isn't necessary to look for scapegoats or to give in to despair or self-blame. Nor is it necessary, as many parents do, to take on the burden of the children's misbehavior—to clean up after them or otherwise cater to their demands. No, there are still a few last-ditch tricks in your bag!

We've frequently advised you that resorting to punishment will undermine your goal of being a good parent. Punishment can set off a chain reaction of mutual hostility, and you'll end up with a round of recriminations and verbal wrestling matches. That's certainly not bargaining—it's feuding!

What's the alternative? Conscientious parents can't afford simply to look the other way when confronted with headstrong youthful rebellion, can they? If they do, they're almost guaranteed to get more of it. After all, you struck a mutually agreed-upon bargain, believing in good faith that both parties would follow through. On some basic level of fairness and justice, you may justifiably feel you *deserve* to have your final agreement honored.

Ignoring broken promises won't do anything to instill in your child that vital sense of responsibility he will need later on in life. Irresponsible people don't fare very well in our modern world. They constantly lose jobs, friends, marriage partners, and financial security, and they often find themselves helpless to deal effectively with the demands of a complex society.

The world has many subtle ways of punishing those who fail to meet their obligations. It may seem preferable to mete out sanctions at home and thereby train a child so that she can avoid even tougher recriminations in the outside world. So an intelligent argument certainly can be made for the importance of requiring children to honor their obligations, even if some form of punitive action is required.

In this chapter we'll look at a few options to apply negative consequences when it seems impossible to control a child's behavior through positive means. But we are going to recommend the *calculated* response—*not* the heated, unplanned response. Let's begin by pointing out what can happen if you use your anger unwisely.

These are the two most destructive by-products of angry punishment:

- The child's increased anxiety from fear of punishment
- The child's active hostility directed toward parents or other available targets

Let's look more closely at these two dangers.

Danger 1. Children who live in frequent fear of punishment experience exaggerated levels of anxiety.

With a dark sense of apprehension, they see an ongoing threat hanging over them like a giant wrecking ball, shadowing their every move. There is the feeling of not measuring up to parental standards and the humiliation of being beaten or treated as an inferior and unworthy person. It's like a domestic Sword of Damocles, ready to drop at the slightest provocation.

Sound a little too dramatic? Not to a child!

A youngster's sense of impending doom will increase significantly if punishment occurs for offenses the child doesn't understand. And abnormal levels of anxiety about punishment over extended periods at an early age tend to follow such children into their adult lives. Youngsters who have been punished tend to abuse their own offspring in the same ways.

Severely punished and abused children may not develop normal levels of self-esteem. They strive unsuccessfully to please various authoritarian figures in their lives. They tremble too much at a frown and are relieved too much by a smile. These youngsters impose on themselves rigid, unreachable standards of behavior, in the hope of being successful and avoiding further punishment. Meanwhile they may grow timid and communicate less, so that parents may not be aware of the damage that punishment—or simply the threat of punishment—is inflicting on their child. Even the affection they show their parents can become a means of fending off parental anger.

One young man came to me after a serious breakdown in high school. He complained of a lack of self-esteem and purpose in his life. On the outside this boy was a model student, and overall he seemed healthy and pleasant. But his achievements gave him no satisfaction, and he was unusually timid. These factors were signals that something serious might be wrong.

Extensive interviews revealed that from the inside looking out, his life was a nightmare of anticipation of failure. He had suffered from years of physical punishment and humiliating treatment inflicted by an insensitive father. Having been unable to please that important figure, he was unable to please himself.

This young man appeared normal into his teen years. It's true he was shy, somewhat compulsive, and stubborn. But he wasn't otherwise remarkable.

Then one day, when he was reprimanded for not turning in a routine history assignment, he simply fell apart. The stress of years of heavy home discipline finally took its toll. His pent-up anxiety exploded when he found he simply couldn't measure up to his impossible standards.

This may seem like an extreme reaction. But this sort of thing occurs all too often in our society. In fact, in less dramatic forms, it may be downright epidemic.

To create such a reaction in a child, punishment need not involve obvious abuse, beatings, or severe and unusual restrictions. Sometimes if a child tends to be rather sensitive, seemingly mild forms of disapproval, if repeatedly and unpredictably applied, may produce such disastrous or near-disastrous results.

Think back on your ways of dealing with your child:

- Do you sometimes give him the silent treatment, perhaps to reinforce your disapproval of his breach of certain behavior standards?
- Do you withhold affection to show your displeasure?
- Do you raise your voice or shout at relatively minor infractions?
- When you respond negatively, do you fail to make it clear to your child what action of his has provoked your response?
- Do you make punishments depend partly, or even largely, upon *your* mood at the time, rather than upon the specific behavior of your child?

Of course all parents lose control occasionally. But the main thing you want to watch for is recurrent destructive patterns in your own behavior. In dealing with families, I'm constantly amazed to discover how often parents don't realize how they are using the kinds of subtle emotional punishments I've listed in the questions just above. Honest answers to those questions are not easy. It's not pleasant to feel that an answer of yes may be required.

It's especially important to become more aware of how your punishment or overt disapproval is affecting your child. Does she dissolve into tears regularly when you correct her? Does a relatively mild reprimand seem to bother her for the rest of the day—or for even longer periods?

In short, it's necessary to determine whether your punishments and sanctions, physical or verbal, are correcting problems or creating them. To this end, it's helpful to examine with great care what you are doing.

Chances are that you're on the wrong track if the punishment you're inflicting is largely an emotional release for your own anger and frustration. As we've seen in previous chapters, there are much better options at your disposal—positive options that can teach your child proper conduct without having his contacts with you become the stuff of nightmares.

Danger 2. Punishment may create hostility in your child.

Children who feel oppressed by a parent will frequently take out their frustration on something or someone else. They won't necessarily go directly after the parent. If they do, they know they'll just receive additional and probably more severe punishment in return. Instead they choose a time or a target where they can vent their hostility with less fear of the consequences.

One extreme case I encountered involved a six-year-old boy who was constantly getting into mischief around the home. His mother decided to implement a pattern of spanking every time he misbehaved. Unfortunately she ended up spanking him several times a day. Also, she wasn't consistent, and the boy became confused about his transgressions. The child seemed to the parent to be growing more and more indifferent to the punishment. But that wasn't what was happening. In fact, the spanking was causing anger to build up in the youngster. He couldn't retaliate immediately against his mother because that would have simply meant more spanking. So he acted indirectly.

For example, he urinated on the front steps when she wasn't around. He broke his sister's toys and slapped her when he thought his mother wasn't free to intervene. He stole cookies from the cookie box. In these ways he could express his hostility without having to confront immediate threats of additional punishment. Unfortunately for him, his mother sometimes discovered the infraction, and the punishment might follow anyway on those occasions.

The first step in finding an answer to the problem in this home was for the mother to abandon spanking as her main means of control. Then she needed to try a more positive means of getting the boy to behave.

In this case, we agreed to change her reaction to the boy's infractions, and then we set up a token system with rewards that appealed to the boy. We made sure that the boy understood what the mother expected from him, and that he would become entitled to the rewards when he acted in a way that was consistent with his mother's wishes.

A dangerous situation also arises when a child chooses to take revenge on a living target that is more vulnerable than himself. For example, one teenage boy regularly received severe punishment from his parents for various rule infractions. But then, when he was assigned to supervise or play with his younger brothers and sisters, he would punish them quite harshly when they didn't play according to his rules.

The boy's father could never quite pinpoint these offenses so that he would have a clear reason to discipline the boy for them. As a result, the youngster developed a very unsatisfactory way of dealing with people weaker than himself.

The answer here was not simply to stop the boy's play with other youngsters, because that would have been treating the symptom rather than the cause. Instead, with some success, we began to eliminate the frequency of parental punishment for bad behavior and substitute rewards for good behavior.

In another case, a young mother was alarmed when she found several small bruises on her six-month-old daughter. One day she passed the nursery door in her home just in time to see her three-year-old daughter reach out and pinch the infant.

After further investigation, the mother learned that the older child tried to punish the baby more frequently at times when she herself had been reprimanded. The baby was defenseless and became an obvious target for the three-year-old, who wanted to get back at her mother, the real source of the child's hostility.

In most homes where punishment is practiced, children are not this troubled. But if there's any risk of such side effects of punishment, that's too high a price to pay. For that matter, anything that disrupts the loving environment in your home is too high a price to pay. Parents who value the emotional health and welfare of their children *must* look for other solutions.

But sometimes something will go wrong with a bargain you've worked out with your child, and no renegotiations seem to work. For example, your oldest child may persist in stealing toys from other children. What are you supposed to do? It's difficult to arrange a negotiated agreement for a problem behavior when you can't easily discover whether or not, or even when, it occurs. Do you just throw up your hands and let him run wild? Who's the ultimate boss in your family —you or your child? That's the next question we need to consider in deciding what to do with a bargain that breaks down.

140

WHO'S THE BOSS?

Who's the boss? For all our emphasis on negotiation, it's still clear that you are—no question about that. As the parent, you're the one who's ultimately in charge.

At the same time, however, you want to produce loving, lovable, responsible children who will develop into responsible adults. You *don't* want to turn out broken-spirited humanoids. So being the boss in the family isn't synonymous with becoming a domestic dictator.

In any family, there's a pendulum of parent-child relations that swings back and forth between permissiveness and prohibition. The great trick in child-rearing is to keep that pendulum swinging very gently, where Fairness, Flexibility, Friendliness, and Firmness prevail in your relationship with your youngster. Remember: Those Four Fs are the key attitudes to keep in mind during negotiation with kids.

When the pendulum swings too far to the left, you approach that dangerous territory of excessive *permissiveness.* That's when a parent allows the child to call the shots. There are many rationalizations and justifications for overpermissiveness. They come into play particularly when you are looking for reasons to give up on a disciplinary attempt. And, indeed, they will often have much merit. Here are a few that may be all too familiar to you:

- You don't want to disturb your child's natural creativity.
- You don't want to infringe on his rights.
- You want to avoid disturbing his emotional stability.
- You want to keep the peace and avoid public scenes.
- You don't want to be unreasonable when your child makes excuses for not keeping his bargains.

The problem is that parents who are too permissive have abandoned their influence over the destiny of their child. And permissive adults are highly vulnerable to being manipulated by their children. A host of negative character traits may be fostered in a permissive atmosphere—and the ultimate goal of developing a well-behaved, responsible child gets further and further out of reach.

On the other hand, as the pendulum swings to the far right, we move into an equally dangerous area of excessive *prohibition,* or what psychologists might call overcontrol. Here we find, at the extreme, adherence to that time-worn adage "Children should be seen and not heard." Children in this sort of environment are supposed to do as they're told and to suffer the consequences if they don't.

Ironically children who labor under a plethora of prohibitions are often expected to act like grownups. But the restrictive environment in which they find themselves doesn't do much to teach them how acting grown-up is going to be of any benefit to them. They may be good workers, but they won't be good managers. They are left unprepared for taking over the reins of control in their own lives as they get older. They lack the tools and skills required to be productive, self-assured adults—even though they may be quite well-mannered and responsible.

To cultivate an atmosphere conducive to ongoing negotiations in your family, you have to stay away from both extremes. It's necessary to stay in the middle area, where Fairness, Flexibility, Friendliness, and Firmness prevail. In this region you remain a benevolent "boss." At the same time, your child has sufficient freedom to engage in give-and-take with you and to develop those abilities that will help turn her into a responsible, confident adult.

You still may be unable to avoid a dilemma. Even though your home atmosphere may be just right for effective negotiations, with a friendly environment and willingness to bargain—things may still go awry. After all, there are many influences on your children that are outside your knowledge and control, and these may be very powerful. They are everywhere—at school, in books, on television, and wherever your child goes. So, finally, you may find that you have an irretrievably broken bargain, and now you want to know what you can do about it.

Let's consider some ways that punishment can be considered when all positive methods have been exhausted. First of all, the major features of properly applied punishment are:

• Be totally clear and consistent about when and how punishment is to be applied.

• Provide a positive consequence for situations where your child controls his misbehavior and chooses a more desirable line of conduct.

• Avoid anger and emotional expressions that may arouse hostility, whether it's before, during, or after the punishment is applied.

• Remember always that it's important for punishment to be delivered only when it's been clearly announced by preliminary discussions with the child. Negative sanctions should never come unannounced or for infractions that the child doesn't understand.

With these thoughts in mind, let's turn now to some suggestions about some mild but effective forms of punishment that you may use in combination with the positive methods of managing your child's behavior.

THE TOKEN-COST SOLUTION

Your daughter has started using obscene and profane language, and there seems to be nothing you can do to get her to stop. Attempts to negotiate a program of rewards simply don't succeed in controlling her habit. She says she forgets.

So what can you do?

One possibility is to negotiate a kind of negative token system. It works this way:

You give your daughter—quite freely—ten points every day. Then you subtract one for every vulgar word or phrase you hear her use, up to the daily total of ten. For every subtraction, you agree to gently and briefly tell her what you have done in response to the words she has used. To be successful, though, you'll have to take away no more than one point when you hear a string of forbidden words in a short time period.

Even at her worst, she almost never would exceed ten such words or phrases in a day. So you and she are sure she will almost always win some points every day. And remember, as we advised earlier, the child should never go below zero. Set up the program so that isn't allowed to happen. The points can later be used for various treats and activities.

As you can see, this approach involves imposing penalties for unacceptable behavior. But at least it starts out positively with those free ten points, and it's highly unlikely that your youngster will begin to use so much vulgar language that she'll fall into the zero-point category.

IGNORING BAD CONDUCT

Suppose your youngsters get involved in constant quarrels, and you've found yourself thwarted at every turn in trying to get them to stop. Negotiations have failed. The children seem to forget their agreement when their play gets too intense and exciting.

Paradoxically the best response to such quarreling may be doing nothing. It seems amazing to many parents, but research studies have repeatedly shown that children *sometimes* will reduce or cease their quarreling if the parents stop trying to act as mediators and ignore the spats.

Quarreling can apparently serve as a call for parental sympathy or just for attention, even if that attention is given roughly. In fact, children who seek this kind of response may be very much in need of more pleasant parental interactions. When pleasant responses aren't available, we know that children are often willing to take whatever they can get.

So as a first approach for minor quarrels, you might just try ignoring them! You'll have to do it for quite a few quarrels, though, before the children learn that you are no longer an automatic "mediation service."

Look also at how much time you're devoting to play and other pleasant interactions with your children. Do you read to them regularly and have other happy experiences with them? If you find that it's mainly your children's *misbehavior* that makes you more attentive to them, it's no wonder you get so much rebellious, unacceptable conduct from them!

TIME-OUT!

You've done everything you can to negotiate and renegotiate an agreement. And generally speaking, things are going rather well. But inevitably, crisis situations are going to develop. In extreme circumstances, children forget themselves and their agreements, and they let their emotions get out of hand—just as you or I.

These situations occur in almost every family: tantrums, shouting, sassing, fighting, and similar obnoxious behavior. The fine points of a negotiated agreement your child has made will be lost on him when he has dropped to the floor, weeping and wailing and kicking. You may be something close to a "super parent" and your offspring may be quite remarkable, but you're still going to encounter this sort of behavior on occasion.

What parent hasn't heard those unloving words "I hate you!" Or "No, I don't care, I'm not going to do it!" The variations are virtually endless. Usually your child is telling you, "I want this very badly—and until I get it, we're both going to suffer." Furthermore, if this approach works, the youngster will learn a very poor method of negotiating. So giving in here is not your best bet. What do you do?

A much better response that often succeeds in such situations is "time out." Here's how it works: Suppose your son and daughter, Tom and Patty, are playing peacefully as they agreed to do a few days ago. But then an argument begins. The decibel level rises as tempers flare.

It's obvious that neither Tom nor Patty is remembering the previous bargain not to fight. Their emotions are running so high that they're not exactly open to reason. So it's time for you to intervene, not to negotiate, but to call a time-out.

You just say, "Time-out!" and then you send (or take) each child to a neutral corner, so to speak. Specifically, you have each of the youngsters go quietly to some separate, uninteresting place for a specified amount of time. They have to stay there without speaking or entertaining themselves until the time is up.

This approach often works like a charm. Why is time out so effective? First, it disrupts the problem. Schoolteachers have been using this approach for years. Remember when an unruly child was put in the corner for a while? That's time-out in action, a time-tested technique to stop the disruption dead in its tracks.

Second, a child will quickly learn that time out is no fun. The message: Getting into situations that result in being isolated from others is not too profitable. It's a punishment, yet it's a mild one. Furthermore, time out is a much more reasonable solution for parents than is physical or verbal abuse. When you decide to use time-out, here are a few guidelines to follow:

Guideline 1. Don't stop to determine blame when you intervene.

If you have made it clear that a certain behavior is not acceptable, then it isn't necessary, or desirable, to discuss the question before using time out. Just state calmly *why* you are doing what you are doing; don't elaborate, repeat, or argue. If you try to assess who was at fault after an argument between two children, for example, each child will have his own report: "John pulled my hair!" "But Jane scratched my arm first!" Your decision to allocate blame may well be the wrong one.

Who is at fault need not be an issue when children are actively disruptive. In effect, time-out is a sure-fire, no-fault-insurance response for a parent when a child begins to get out of hand. You simply retire each child to a separate place to serve his time. If two quarrelers are thus separated, they will be less likely in the future to retaliate against one another if they know that *both* are sure to face the same sanction.

Guideline 2. Put the child in an uninteresting place.

It isn't really effective to send a child to his bedroom where he can play with his toy trains or listen to his stereo. Obviously a time-out place that has a television, books, toys, or anything else that makes the time interesting, won't work. Often the best place for time-out is a relatively uncomfortable chair, with no opportunity for distracting activity.

A bathroom may also be a good place—just so long as your child isn't too creative. One little girl I know amused herself there by using her mommy's cold cream and powder to mix a "witch's brew." Then there was the inventive little boy who dressed himself in toilet paper—using the entire roll! Another boy learned to wet wads of toilet paper and throw it against the bathroom walls, where it would stick in interesting arrangements. You'll have to be creative, too, if your child tries to defeat your program by these means.

The same problem exists in finding a properly isolated spot for older children and teens. I've seen otherwise intelligent teachers who make the same mistake over and over again, without ever seeming to catch on. They force a misbehaving student to sit in the hall—supposedly where there's nothing to do. But then that student can entertain himself by chatting with everyone who passes by, and he also avoids his unpleasant arithmetic lesson. The hallway turns out to be a more interesting spot than the classroom.

The class may get along better without the offending student's disruption, but the time-out spot isn't isolated enough to give him sufficient opportunity to reflect upon his misdeeds.

You have to use your judgment according to what you know about your child's ideas for entertaining himself. The general idea is to make that time-out period less rewarding than the activity the child is being taken away from.

Guideline 3. Set a limited amount of time for the period of time out.

Remember: You're not banishing the child from your presence permanently. You just want to make life less rewarding for her temporarily. It's also important to keep in mind your child's concept of time. For young children, five minutes can seem an infinite period. But the older a youngster gets, the longer the time out should become.

On the other hand, you don't want to leave any child in an isolated place for a very extended period. I've seen children kept out of circulation so long that they begin to suffer from a lack of productive human contact and the opportunity to pursue normal learning activities. So use your good judgment in selecting an appropriate duration. In general I recommend a maximum of fifteen minutes of time-out for very young children, though one minute is often enough. And there should be no more than an hour for teens.

But what if your child throws a major tantrum or rage and the outburst continues after you put time-out into effect, and continues even when the time runs out?

Wait a few moments. Then inform the youngster that his time-out period will end shortly after his fit is over. Do this once, briefly and quietly. Anything more will defeat your purpose. In other words, resist the urge to try to persuade your child to quiet down; if you try persuasion or arguments, you'll just make things worse.

After your one brief statement, keep him sitting there in

that uninteresting place until he's finally quieted down. Then, after a minute or so, say, "Okay, now your time is up."

In any case, don't keep the child in isolation longer than your maximum period. When the period has ended, if he still shows a high degree of anger, just tell him he can stay out as long as he controls himself, and release him.

Guideline 4. Be firm away from home.

If your child misbehaves away from home, you may have some difficult social problems. But it's still important to be consistent, even when you're a guest somewhere.

If you're visiting good friends or relatives, it may be appropriate to use your time-out technique right on the spot. You may have to explain what you are doing so they can cooperate. Most likely they know you well and will be accommodating as you look for an uninteresting place in their home.

On the other hand, if you're in a grocery store, for example, or with some casual acquaintances or strangers, you may need to be creative. Try using a coatroom, bathroom, or hallway. Or put the child's coat over his head for a brief time.

If your child's outbursts are too offensive, your ultimate resort may be to leave, sit in the car awhile, or go home. Or you might retire to some nearby place where a time-out procedure is possible. Your child probably won't really want to leave, and when you threaten to go, he'll immediately begin to behave properly. But if he persists, I think it's important just to leave.

After one or two experiences of having to leave a festive atmosphere and sit alone in a boring setting for a while, the child is likely to reconsider his behavior. He'll begin to realize that causing trouble is no fun, and he'll also understand that you're serious about dealing with his troublemaking. But don't use this form of time-out if you feel your child would prefer to leave.

Be careful not to show anger or hostility when you use time-out, even if your child shows anger. Instead just be cool and calm, with a minimum of comment. No sermons or criticisms.

Guideline 5. Don't compensate your child for the time-out.

When a time-out session is over, it's helpful to give your youngster a *very* brief explanation of why you had to use discipline. But no more. Providing an ice cream cone and perhaps an extended discussion of why you responded as you did are no-nos! Don't try to resolve your guilt this way! Giving your child extra attention after the time out could cancel its effect.

But after the time-out, a sign of affection is very appropriate. Don't become a "refrigerator parent" as a further punishment! All is forgiven, and you are ready to be an openly loving parent again.

Guideline 6. Don't argue with your child about using a time-out.

If your child is in the midst of a tantrum when you decide to use time out, it's likely that you'll bear some of the brunt of his verbal hostility. He may try to argue with you, or he may even begin to shout insults. Whatever his reaction, it's best to let his remarks fly right by you with no response. Just stay calm and remove him to a quiet place where you can implement the time-out procedure.

Entering into an argument with the child at this point

won't accomplish anything, except perhaps to escalate the anger you both may be feeling. If you engage in an argument or discussion each time before you put a time-out into effect, that may actually become an interaction that your child looks forward to. He may sense that by drawing you into the conflict he's exercising some hostile "countercontrol"—and that's precisely one of the things that you want to avoid.

Guideline 7. Build the time-out program into your negotiations.

When you're negotiating an agreement, you might include the use of time out as a mutually agreed-upon procedure. Then when a time-out is employed the child may still complain, but his previous agreement should reduce his hostility.

To summarize, time out can be used for any crisis situation when you feel you should step in immediately:

- You use it when your child is persistently acting contrary to his agreements.
- You use it when two or more children are quarreling.
- You use it when a child's emotions have gone completely out of control.
- Using time out doesn't mean you don't negotiate about your child's difficulties afterward. It just says to the child, "Your method of getting your way isn't going to work. You'll have to learn a better way!"

Bargains are going to be broken from time to time. But now you have the tools to handle most situations that will confront you as responsible parents. First, of course, you should look for possible ways to renegotiate. If all else fails, you can fall back on a form of "time out" to sanction your child.

Using such approaches, you'll be in the best position to continue effective communication with your child, and you'll also minimize the possibilities for resentment to arise and fester. Before long you'll discover that your hard-to-manage child is finally turning into the responsible, self-disciplined adult that you'd always been hoping for.

As you might expect, this ultimate result doesn't happen overnight. A great deal of creative negotiating must go on before the average child is transformed into the ideal adult. Parents must be especially sensitive to the need of their children to be treated as individuals. In other words, they have to understand that different kids mean different deals.

Different Kids Need Different Deals

S*OMETIMES* there seem to be as many variations in children as there are in snowflakes. My years as a clinical psychologist have convinced me that children are a lot alike, but it's their differences that make them most interesting. In some way, every child is different from any other.

But not only is every child a little different from the next; every *parent* is different, too. As a result, when a particular parent is dealing with a particular child, there are no foolproof, overriding formulas that will give complete answers for every problem. You must first have knowledge of some basic principles of child-rearing. You also must expect the unexpected. You have to be ready to "go with the flow" and react to new challenges on the spot, with a sense of the excitement and adventure that goes with continual novelty.

As far as negotiation with children is concerned, what all this boils down to is that different kids require different deals. But what exactly does this mean in practice?

Before we get into the nitty-gritty of some specific negotiations, let's take a detailed look at the three fundamental factors that make the bargaining in one home different from the bargaining in the next.

Difference 1. Each child is unique.

You may hear another parent say, "My Johnny is so strong willed! But I've found a way to deal with him . . ."

Your Timmy may be just as strong willed. But even that doesn't mean that your friend's solution is going to work in your home too.

Granted you may learn some important things from the experience of others. In fact I make that very assumption in presenting the various principles and practical situations in this book. You *can* learn a great deal from other people's experience, including their successes and failures.

At the same time it's essential to remember your own child's individuality. He has special motives; he responds to special incentives; and he has his own special sensitivities and stubborn streaks. He was born different, and he has lived different. No other child was ever exactly like him.

In short, you can't force a solution on one child, even though it may have worked quite well with another. A bargain or reward system that worked well for another child may be one your child won't respond to at all. It will be as tricky and dangerous as an old banana peel: without any nutritional value, and likely to cause a slip-up!

Perhaps you've never taken the time to sit down with a pencil and paper and muse about your child's distinctive characteristics. Such a list might start anywhere, but certain characteristics are particularly important in planning a negotiation.

For example, you should know what activities he enjoys.

Just writing down what he does with his free time is a good start. Don't forget the time he shares with his friends and family members. What food does he enjoy? Does he collect things? What sort of music, books, sports, or people does he find appealing?

What are his reactions to you and to other people? Does he like to please? Is he stubborn when crossed? Or does he sulk or become insulting? Is he attentive and thoughtful? Does he plan his actions, or is he precipitous—or both?

Be sure to list his strengths; don't concentrate on deficiencies. Because there's much you have to be thankful for, don't just list abstract characteristics. If you think your child is generous, for instance, try to recall some specifics. Do the examples have anything in common? Also, if you think he's sometimes dishonest, think of some examples.

You know better than anyone what's going on with your child. If you put your knowledge together, specifically and exactly, your youngster should emerge as a distinctive little human being, different from anyone else in the world. And you should understand better just *how* he differs so that you can negotiate more effectively with him.

Difference 2. Parents are different, too.

Each parent subscribes to a particular set of ideals, standards, and goals in life that he wants to instill in his children. We share these views to a degree with the people around us, certainly; but there are differences in the type of beliefs we have, and in the intensity with which we hold them.

It's at this point that problems frequently appear. Parents are unsure about what they want for their children. What is best? What's possible? Do I want too much, or too little? As a result, parents often tend to be weak and inconsistent in setting goals for their children.

Suppose, for example, that you notice your daughter has been picking up vulgar language from her schoolmates. This doesn't seem to you to be a very healthy development. You know she hears it every day, but you are embarrassed to hear how unwisely she uses it around you and your friends. So you decide to work out an arrangement that will discourage your child from using such language.

Among other things, you tell her, "It's ill-mannered and just plain wrong to use such language, so I want to reward you when you go a whole day without using any bad words."

You don't want to use punishment for this problem, so you and your daughter proceed to negotiate a system whereby she'll receive some reward for staying away from bawdy and profane language.

Unfortunately the whole deal falls apart. Why? Because *you* have a vulgar mouth yourself! As soon as you've completed your negotiations, you turn right around and let loose with one of the very curse words that you've tried to negotiate out of your daughter's vocabulary! Her tendency to model herself after you is too great to be overcome by the reward system you've set up.

There are several problems with this sort of situation. First of all, the parent is providing a poor role model for the child. Even though the adult is a bad role model, it might still be possible for a negotiation to take care of the problem. After all, children learn early that what is permitted to parents is often not permitted to the children. But your poor modeling is certainly making the problem more difficult. So it might be best for you to make *your own* reformation a part of the deal.

On an even more basic level, a parent with this problem

shows that he hasn't quite made up his own mind about the meaning of that bad language. Is it *really* bad? Is it only bad for kids? Is it a fault you can't cure in yourself, even though you want to change it in your child?

Children simply can't deal with such fine distinctions. "If it's okay for you, why isn't it okay for me?" they wonder. In a sense this becomes a case of "physician, heal thyself." In any case, it's fairly obvious here that the parent may well not have a clear idea about just what is good for his child.

So before you can deal with your child effectively in a negotiated situation, you have to deal with your own special differences on at least two levels: (1) you must decide what those differences really are, and (2) you'll need to deal with some basic questions about your own value system and the inconsistencies in it.

Difference 3. Your children are evolving as individuals.

Even as you acknowledge that your child is different from any other, you must also recognize that she is constantly changing. As she gets older and perhaps moves with you to other cities and is exposed to different social situations, she'll inevitably change.

You'll therefore have to allow for periodic reevaluations of who your child is and what motivates her. You'll have to ask, "Has she outgrown that old agreement? Is it time to reopen negotiations, now that she's a year older?"

The answer to these and similar questions often will be yes. Times change, and so do kids. So one of your major goals is to keep step with this developing little being and nudge her in one direction or another as she gets older.

That's one of the beauties of the negotiating process: You

have a means to keep in constant touch with your child's changing motives, needs, and challenges. The *same* child is going to require different approaches over the years as he evolves into an adult, and you can devise the most effective approaches by coming up with corresponding deals.

With these fundamental factors in mind, let's now move on to some specific situations that typical families face these days. As you'll see, each of these sets of circumstances can be found in one form or another in most families. But the way the specifics work out in practice is very individual.

SIBLING SQUABBLES

Sometimes parents feel they have discovered that it's a basic law of the universe that brothers and sisters must bicker constantly, if only to give their parents something to do. Otherwise the parents would be able to live in too much peace and tranquillity—and this is simply not the way the world is supposed to operate. If I specialized in fantasy, I could believe this, too. But the world does not conspire against us. It's more accurate to say we conspire against ourselves.

True, siblings often quarrel. But the reasons for those quarrels are rooted in the same kinds of concerns, upsets, and personal deficiencies that plague adults. Combativeness seems to come easily to human beings, young or old. When we're older, we control and channel our combativeness better, but the young usually show it in less civilized ways.

Like anyone else, growing children often discover that their wishes are in direct conflict with those of someone else. And the someone who is often the source of contention is a sibling. After all, brothers and sisters must share the same living space, bathroom time, material possessions, and telephone systems. They also have to share the attention of their parents—and that can be the most explosive factor of all.

There are as many grounds for combat among siblings in the average American home as there were among nations in World War II. The sooner you as a parent accept this state of affairs, the sooner you'll be able to go about resolving the conflicts.

There are usually two distinct roles that the parent must play in dealing with sibling squabbles. First, the parent as *peacemaker* has to step in to stop the argument or fight when it threatens to escalate out of control. Second, the parent as *mediator* should calculate carefully how mediation can best be accomplished. Then he should move to negotiate a mutual agreement between the warring parties.

Role 1: Peacemaker. If the quarreling won't subside just by ignoring it, you might chose to try the time-out procedure that we've discussed in Chapter 7. Time out centers on stopping the out-of-control quarrel dead in its tracks. When you decide you must step in as the all-powerful parent, you might quickly move to defuse the situation by separating the children: Put them in spots where they can cool down for a while.

One child, for example, was playing with some toys when his older brother came along and snatched them away. No doubt the younger brother had irritated his older sibling somewhere along the line. That's how feuding usually starts.

By the time the father arrived on the scene, the younger brother was crying and the older one was screaming at him. This was no time for cool-headed negotiations. The stage was set to implement phase one for settling this outbreak.

The father didn't stop to try to assess blame. Instead he immediately took each child and placed him in an isolated spot, away from the other and also from toys or other interesting items to play with.

Of course the conflict between the two was not resolved immediately. In fact the father knew it would erupt again if nothing was done to correct the situation. More use of time out might have ended the quarreling, but this father didn't want to use time out without trying a positive approach. Now the stage was set for the father to assume his second role as mediator.

Role 2: Mediator. The father had come up with some ideas about why the boys quarreled so often. The younger boy was actually more inventive than the older, and he made more constructive and interesting use of the toys. Then the older one would want to use those toys himself in the new form of play that his younger sibling had discovered. So he would try to take the younger boy's toys away. Understanding this difference between the boys helped the father work out his mediation plan.

After a minute or so, the two children had calmed down enough to engage in a three-way conversation with their father about the incident. So the father brought them back together for a bargaining session. Without referring to which youngster was to blame for the argument, he focused on the future. "You both want to play with your toys, right?" he began.

They both said yes, but each tried to make arguments about who owned what, who had first choice, or exclusive choice, and so on. The father, however, cut them off before they could take this line of discussion too far. "All these toys belong to the *both* of you, as I recall," he said. "Isn't that right? Your own special toys are in your rooms." Both acknowledged this was so. So the father continued, "Okay, let's figure out a way to allow each of you to use the toys in a fair way."

As the boys began to discuss the problem more rationally, they eventually agreed that whoever was playing with a toy had the right to continue until he agreed freely to turn it over to the other. The father said that if he was called in to mediate, he would always ask the boys to go to their rooms to cool off. He would not try to settle their disagreements for them.

The father also set up a reward for peaceful play by using a token system that was already in effect in the home for some of their other behavior. He said to the firstborn that he felt that since the boy was older, he should be responsible for his younger brother's peaceful play. So the parent offered the older youngster a greater reward than he offered the younger one. The younger child agreed to this because he realized he would more often have undisturbed play.

In this situation, the father couldn't fall back on any cut-and-dried formula to resolve the conflict. He had to assess the particular interests and personalities of the two people that he was dealing with and then make his suggestions in light of those facts. He had to come up with a special deal for his special kids.

Another case of sibling rivalry, which was much more complicated than the one we've just considered, demonstrates the variations on a theme there can be in different homes.

Sally and Jack were school-age siblings, twelve and fourteen years old respectively, and both had to study for important final exams. So they settled down in the family room to work, one at a desk and the other on the floor by the stereo.

Jack liked to study with the music on, and he cranked up his tape deck to full volume. Sally, a more serious student, preferred the quiet of a library. Hence the stage was set for a battle royal.

Sally began by demanding that Jack's music be turned off, but her younger brother refused. He claimed he could concentrate just fine without being distracted by the music. And he wasn't about to change his style just to suit her.

A raucous shouting match exploded across the tranquil landscape of this home. Ignoring them didn't work. The mother had tried this before in previous battles. When the mother finally decided to intervene, it was obvious that some type of Role 1 intervention would have to be implemented.

So this mother stepped in to stop the quarrel from escalating. But she decided a time-out wouldn't work. The problem needed another solution. The mother told Sally and Jack to sit down. Then, in soothing terms, without blaming either of them for anything, she explained that something would have to be done about their quarreling over this issue.

Finally, with things now relatively quiet, the parent and the two children began in a more rational way to examine their problem. Their quandary was how to reach an agreement acceptable to both, without giving one an advantage over the other.

This may not sound too difficult in the abstract. But you may be thinking of solutions for your home that would not have been suitable in this one. For this parent, the problem presented a very difficult challenge.

The negotiating phase got into full swing as the mother allowed the two siblings to discuss possible settlements. First Jack suggested that Sally should go to her bedroom to study. "It'll be much quieter there," he said helpfully—yet with more than a touch of self-interest. Sally rejected that suggestion. She accurately pointed out that the music played at the volume Jack preferred could be heard halfway down the street.

Sally proposed instead that the music be turned off completely during study time. Predictably Jack didn't go for that idea. He argued that having the music on drowned out background noise. Therefore, he argued, the music actually should help Sally study better. Of course Sally was unimpressed by this generous thought.

Turning the music off didn't seem a possibility, so Sally said, "Why don't you use earphones?"

"Because I can't move about as easily on the floor," her brother replied. He explained that he could only study effectively when he stretched out on the floor and rolled about. He spread all his study materials around him, and somehow they always took up half the floor. The earphones got in his way when he was studying this way.

By this point the mother was beginning to get the picture. This brother and sister were definitely not going to settle the issue by themselves for one simple reason—they were at war! They didn't *want* to agree. Both wanted to win! Clearly it was time for the parent-mediator to become more active.

A natural parental reaction in this situation would have been to try *imposed arbitration.* In other words, the mother could have said, "Okay, you two can't agree. So this is the way it's going to be . . ." And then she could have outlined a solution and insisted that the two children go along with it.

But that would have defeated the purpose of negotiation. The children would not have had any significant input into the final settlement. If they had gone along with such a solution, they would merely have been bending to authoritarian rule. The result would most likely have been at best a short-term, uneasy peace.

Sometimes authoritarian rule may be the only answer. But it's only appropriate as a *final* solution, when all other possible avenues of deal making have been exhausted. In any case, it's always important to proceed with caution before you ring the bell on the various contestants and impose your will by brute parental force.

Mom decided that Sally and Jack were not yet at the end of the list of possibilities in their discussion. They were certainly butting heads and refusing to agree with one another, but Mom still felt that a little parental guidance and positive persuasion could get them onto the right track.

The mother understood this and used the impasse that the siblings had reached to give some gentle instruction on the art and importance of compromise. She said that it was obvious that neither of the children would be able to impose his will on the other, and that it was essential for them to reach a meeting of the minds.

Still, she said in calm but firm tones, if they couldn't reach a solution between themselves, she would have to make the decision herself. In other words, she let them know that she would stand in the background as the court of last resort and would impose a solution only if they couldn't make up their minds themselves. Furthermore, she said, any solution they came up with together would probably be more attractive to both of them than something she decided for them.

"We're facing a situation where neither of you is going to win completely," the mother said. "At the same time, neither of you will lose, either, if you'll just put your heads together and come up with an answer."

To get the discussion going again, the mother tossed out a few extra points for consideration. First of all, she said, it did seem that the music was quite loud. Both she and her husband had talked about asking Jack to turn it down. So no matter what the two children decided, Jack should lower the volume.

At the same time, she said, from the parents' point of view there was nothing that dictated Jack should turn the music off entirely. That was something that he and his sister would have to settle between themselves—if they could do so without fighting.

The discussion went on for some time, with no resolution in sight, and everyone steadily became more frustrated. Finally the mother recognized that the problem centered on the fact that Jack was going to have to give up something, but Sally didn't stand to lose anything. Jack would have to give Sally a quieter environment for her study, but she wasn't giving him anything in return. Jack wasn't going to be willing to agree to this.

The mother might have offered Jack some compensation using one of the methods we've discussed. But she decided it would be better if Sally made some sort of sacrifice herself. So she brought in an unrelated area of conflict between the two children—an area in which Sally's behavior was particularly offensive to Jack. The mother mentioned that even though Sally was quite conscientious about her schoolwork, she was very sloppy in the bathroom after showering. The wet towels she left on the floor and puddles of soapy water on every flat surface were a source of constant annoyance to her brother. Jack, a meticulous boy, got particularly peeved because Sally regularly used his comb and left telltale hairs in it. But Sally just didn't worry about such things, as long as she herself emerged well-groomed and attractive.

"I know that Sally's bathroom habits annoy you, Jack," the mother said. "So why don't the two of you see if you can link an agreement on the bathroom with an agreement on the study situation?"

Now both children began to show some interest. Jack could see that there would be a mutual benefit for him, and Sally began to see a fairly easy way to get a quieter room for her work.

There's an important distinction here, by the way. When *you* bring in unrelated issues to *help* a negotiation, that can be extremely perceptive and helpful. But don't fall into the trap of bringing in unrelated gripes for no reason, or out of frustration. And if you bring in unrelated gripes that look to your child like a form of character assassination, you will certainly make matters worse.

But in this case, the unrelated issue was introduced in a productive way, as a legitimate bargaining tool. So the children got down to a serious discussion to try to work out their differences, and before long they came up with a solution.

They decided that Jack would use the earphones, even though he had protested their use so vehemently before. The mother was sure his main objection to using them had simply been that Sally *wanted* him to!

Sally, for her part, said that she would clean up after herself in the bathroom that they shared. She also would be particularly careful about not using Jack's comb. Mother agreed to add these changes in behavior to the family's ongoing token system.

Even though the situation involved mutual compromise, both siblings won. Moreover, their agreement solved two problems that had been the cause of many arguments between them. Perhaps most important, this brother and sister learned how effective a compromise can be when both sides are willing to give way. They also learned that negotiation and compromise were part of an important "insurance package" that could keep them from getting burned in the heat of a disagreement.

Obviously, sibling rivalry isn't going to disappear overnight, with a single successful negotiation. Anyone who thinks that is guilty of wishful thinking in the extreme. But by getting children involved in the negotiation process, fighting can be brought under control. Children learn better ways of resolving conflicts. They begin to understand how to live together in harmony and how to reach their own agreements without relying on a parent as mediator.

Here the agreement made use of unique personalities and peculiar circumstances that were distinctive to this particular family. But every agreement must do so. In short, this is just another of many examples that show why it's important to understand that "different kids mean different deals."

The sibling squabbling that we've discussed here is only one of a host of challenges that require special, individualized handling. There are many skills and habits that every healthy, well-adjusted individual must develop if he hopes to stay in good physical and mental shape. These focus on the basic practices of hygiene, grooming, social manners, and morality—the Basic Facts of Civilized Life. But in all of these, the immediate desires of the child are frequently going to run counter to the desires of the parents. That's where the advantages of negotiation make themselves felt.

9.

The Basic Facts of Civilized Life

*M*ANY facts of life confront every parent who is trying to train his child in the ways of the world. First, of course, there are the birds and the bees, with the many implications that accompany transmitting the knowledge of sex to a young, impressionable mind.

Other facts don't get quite as much publicity. But in their own way, they hold just as many perils. These are what I call the Basic Facts of Civilized Life—the all-important health, social, and moral lessons that every well-appointed person must learn and practice.

But it can be very difficult to explain to a busy eight-year-old *why* he has to take a bath regularly . . . or *why* she has to brush her teeth after every meal . . . or *why* it's important for him to comb the knots and kinks out of his tousled hair. From a child's point of view there is no obvious gain.

Some parents try to explain some of the important social reasons for these habits:

• "Your mom's new slipcovers will get dirty if you don't wash your feet. That could cost us a lot of money to get them cleaned."

- "You may develop a rash on your skin if you don't clean the dirt off."
- "You have to eat your cereal so you'll be strong."
- "People may think you're not as pretty as you really are if you don't comb your hair every morning before you go to school."

But if you try pressing some of these reasons upon your youngster, chances are you'll be met with moans and groans rather than ready acquiescence. Unfortunately money, looks, and long-term benefits often mean very little to children. They don't understand the sacrifices and pains associated with parenthood. They live in the here and now, with scant experience of how the world works or how their present behavior will influence their futures. You may hear multiple excuses, like these classic childhood rebuttals: "Not now, Mom. . . ." "Why shouldn't [someone else] do it?" "I don't want to." You may also hear some counterproposals based on the idea that, unlike classmates of your generation, kids nowadays really don't care about dirt and messiness in their friends. Any agile eight-year-old mind can come up with a host of reasonable alternatives to the onerous tasks of traditional hygiene and grooming.

Making reasonable, adult arguments—or issuing threats— probably won't do much to overcome your child's resistance to developing many of these habits. This is especially true if you fail to instill some of these practices in your son or daughter at a very young age, and you end up with long-practiced bad habits to contend with.

I've noticed something about parents who begin to teach their children at age two or three about brushing their teeth, washing their hands after they use the toilet, and other such habits: They tend to be more successful in instilling such hygienic behavior, even *without* special incentives, than those who wait longer. If you catch your child early enough, you can often just usher him over to the lavatory after he's gone to the bathroom, stick his hands under the running water, and then help him dry his hands. Afterward you will need only a few indications of your pleasure and appreciation, and maybe some words about how important it is to "wash the dirty germs off." If you begin early enough, this kind of monitoring procedure can result in good habits, well learned.

I recall one boy whose parents began to use this approach as soon as he was old enough to use the toilet bowl. As a result, the act of washing his hands after he had urinated became so automatic that just before his bath he would use the toilet and wash his hands—even though he was about to get into the tub where he would wash them all over again!

Such routines are a part of our behavior every day. Somehow with no obvious or immediate pressure or payment, we do them without thought. Something sustains them for us, and the same can happen for our children, once the routines have been learned.

On the other hand, as a child gets older, a monitoring procedure doesn't work as well for training. An older child may do what he's told as you stand over him. But when you're no longer present, he will lapse into his old behavior. Parental approval and good advice often seem to lose some of their power when it comes to correcting long-held deficiencies.

So what's the answer?

As with changing other childhood behavior on a permanent basis, the Basic Facts of Civilized Life are an excellent place to try out a system of negotiation and rewards. You, as the leader of the negotiations, can sit down and discuss the importance of a particular aspect of good hygiene or grooming. Then you and your youngster can begin to work toward an agreement—which will include suitable rewards to give the child an incentive to hop into the bathtub, or whatever, without his usual resistance.

But can the reward system really work without having a parent stand over a child all the time, or without having the parent rely at least partly on threats?

You bet it can. A variety of studies have shown that a very successful way to establish good habits in a child—habits he will be inclined to continue on his own—is to rely on positive reinforcement. This adds an incentive for the very young child that the natural and social environments can't supply. But it isn't necessary to continue this system forever. As the child grows older, the external world exerts its own consequences for good habits, and the system you've established can be gradually removed. Children will discover eventually why good hygiene, for example, has its own rewards. Parents of teenagers see this happen as their child discovers that his peers are taking notice of his cleanliness and appearance.

Remember: One of your major objectives is to establish increasing autonomy and independence in your child. By this we don't mean independence from the outside social and physical world but independence from your specific demands and urgings.

You want your child to require as little parental supervision as possible as he gets older. You want him to follow good grooming and hygiene habits without constant nagging and reminders from you. Eventually your influence will fade as your child moves out among his peers, teachers, friends, business associates, and loved ones. Your goal is to develop a responsible young person who is prepared to confront this world successfully on his own.

The negotiating process encourages your child to engage

in certain behavior that will be important later, because he wants to receive some immediate, tangible rewards. As he gets older, he'll be likely to continue this behavior because of the more abstract, less tangible rewards that are present in the adult world.

In later years your son may want to keep his skin clean in order to get rid of those pimples—and make the girls like him better. Or your daughter may find that it's much easier to get a summer job if she goes to an interview in clean, pressed clothes and if she has clean, well-combed hair. They'll learn that what you taught them long ago is important in ways they couldn't understand at the time.

Of course, even as I make all these generalizations, I realize that each child is different. Each will respond in his own special way to tooth brushing, hair combing, or bed making. One child may develop these habits with the lightest parental attention, while another may seem to respond to parental pressure with extreme reluctance. So it's necessary in this area, as in every other, to consider your child's individual traits when you're trying to formulate an approach to changing his behavior.

Tooth brushing provides a good example of how individualized methods have to be used with each child. One seven-year-old boy, Bob, hadn't yet developed a consistent habit of brushing his teeth, and his parents were eager for him to become more independent in this area. But at first they didn't meet with overwhelming success. To begin with, they tried a very adult approach. "You know, you could really develop tooth problems if you don't brush regularly," Bob's father said. "You've already been to the dentist once or twice, and your teeth have been okay. But if you don't take care of them you could get tooth decay, gum disease, all sorts of pain—and it could cost you a lot of money after you get older. Not only that, your breath may not smell too good if you don't brush those teeth regularly."

Bob listened with a bored expression. Dentists were far away, and his breath was of little concern. But he said he'd try to remember to brush his teeth before he left for school in the morning—and then he forgot all about it. No matter how much his father or mother tried to impress on him the ultimate health and social benefits of having a clean mouth, he wasn't impressed—at least not enough to do anything.

This was quite puzzling and frustrating to the parents. They realized that they pursued good dental hygiene and brushed their teeth regularly without thinking about it. They had developed these habits long ago in childhood, and they couldn't understand why their son couldn't do the same.

Gradually the parental frustration built until the father and mother began to fall back on a close monitoring procedure to get Bob to perform up to par with his toothbrush. This method worked as long as they stood over him and occasionally issued threats. He knew there would be negative consequences if he didn't perform this bathroom task, and so he did it.

Often, this method works, but with Bob it didn't. When the parents backed off to see if Bob would continue this practice on his own, he ignored their objectives and went back to his old ways. Their attempts to train by intimidation had failed.

Finally the parents heard about negotiation and the alleged benefits of using a system of rewards, and Bob's mother suggested they give this approach a try. But the idea didn't make any sense at all to the husband. His reaction: "When was the last time anyone rewarded *you* for brushing your teeth? You brush them because you are afraid people will think badly of you if they see your dinner on your teeth."

The wife felt he was partly right. No one explicitly rewarded her for brushing. The best reasons she knew to explain why she brushed her teeth were like her husband's. They wanted to avoid dental problems and be socially acceptable with clean teeth and fresh-smelling breath.

But neither these reasons nor coercion had worked with their son, so they finally agreed to try the negotiating approach. Specifically they sat down with the child and came up with a token system in which he would get a poker chip every time he brushed his teeth without parental nagging or coaxing. After he had accumulated a certain number of chips, he would be entitled to exchange them for various possible rewards. The boy liked this plan and agreed to permit parental inspection of his mouth so they could be sure he had earned his chip. The parents agreed between themselves that if the inspection gave a negative result, they would only comment that their son hadn't earned his chip yet and say nothing more.

The boy wasn't perfect in following this regimen. But he cooperated fairly well. The parents refrained from criticism, as they had agreed. He forgot to brush his teeth only occasionally—lapses that were certainly to be expected. On the whole, the reward system that the parents had set up provided sufficient incentive for him to brush his teeth by himself most mornings and evenings. Eventually, his tooth brushing became automatic, and gradually the token system was discontinued. His parents still would occasionally inspect and praise his performance, and that seemed to be enough.

These parents were able to tailor a negotiated settlement to this boy's particular character. The result was the development of an important hygiene habit that promised to remain deeply ingrained in him throughout adulthood.

A MATTER OF GOOD MANNERS

It's a typical Wednesday afternoon—and Mom's day off from work. She's in the kitchen when daughter Jane comes home from school, and there's a freshly baked cake on the counter.

The cake is intended primarily for guests the family is expecting that evening for dinner. But it's also a family favorite. And Jane, who has a sweet tooth, is especially hungry after a long day at school. So she decides to see if she can get a little advance on that dessert.

"Hi, Mom," she says. "May I please have a piece of cake?"

"Sure, honey. I made your favorite kind. Just don't forget to put your plate in the dishwasher when you're finished."

"Thanks, Mom."

"You're welcome, Jane."

Sound like a scene from that old TV show *Father Knows Best?* Not at all!

This is simply an example of a loving family that understands how to integrate good manners into practical discussions. In fact, what's taken place between Jane and her mother is an informal negotiation that has been made more palatable and effective by the use of polite language and conduct. And now you can see that you've been negotiating with your children all along! Let's look at how this negotiation went.

First of all, Mom has baked a cake that both Jane and the rest of the family love. In part that was a small gesture to tell Jane that she's important. At the same time, Jane has learned that her relationship with her mother proceeds most smoothly when she prefaces any request with that magic word "please."

In making this particular request, Jane is also opening the door to an on-the-spot, informal kind of negotiation with her mother. She knows from past experience that by making a request in a polite way, she's more likely to get a positive response.

It's important to understand that there's nothing calculating or manipulative in Jane's approach. She is not trying to get something for nothing. Her request arises from genuine feelings of love and mutual appreciation between the mother and daughter. Mom is well rewarded by Jane's appreciative response.

In effect Jane's well-mannered request constitutes a kind of offer to her mother. On one level, she's saying, "Mom, I'd like something you have, and if I get it, I'll make your day by showing my love and how much your gesture has pleased me!"

The mother's response? She accepts: "Sure, Honey."

But she also includes a condition with her acceptance—one about which she and her daughter have apparently reached an understanding in the past. The girl must do more to show her pleasure and love than smile and be grateful. She must also show that she will return care for care, by cleaning up after herself.

So what is the girl's response to this suggested deal? She agrees: "Thanks, Mom."

Not just an "okay." But a much more polite "Thanks." Once again, polite expressions smooth the way to a productive interchange between mother and daughter. This is not just a way of achieving selfish means. Each party benefits from this interaction. The "please" and "thanks" and the help with the dishes reflect mutual love and respect on the part of mother and daughter.

The final step in this simple exchange is a kind of polite

icing on the cake, so to speak, as the mother indicates that she has been amply repaid: "You're welcome, Jane."

All these steps are important. Jane and her mother are *not* just being polite. They are exchanging favors and rewards that are an important part of their ongoing smooth relationship.

But the important thing is that your child learns what constitutes good manners and courtesy in his or her particular social and family context. It's essential for the youngster to realize that good manners are a means of expressing love and respect to another person, and also a way of making social interactions proceed more smoothly and pleasantly.

Some children have not developed essential social graces, and they fail to express their appreciation toward their parents and others. For example, a child may take parental love and displays of affection for granted. He may not understand that it's important to return those expressions of love with appropriate words of gratitude. His parents are missing out on one of the important rewards of parenthood. So it's up to them to fill in the gaps in their child's development and teach him how to be polite and courteous.

There are two good ways that children learn manners in the home.

Method 1: Training through Imitation. This first way to learn manners involves imitation or patterning behavior after that of the parents. The process should begin at a very early age with "please" and "thank you."

If a parent consistently uses words like *please, thank you,* and *you're welcome,* the child may learn by observation to do likewise. If he doesn't, the parent can remind him, beginning in toddlerhood. To train a child to say "please" you might start very early. When your child makes a request, you say, "Don't you want to say the magic word?" Or perhaps just looking inquiringly at him for the word will do, after he has had some early successes.

If *you* always say "please" when you make requests, that will make your child even more likely to do the same. It's difficult for some parents to thank their children and acknowledge their efforts. Some adults don't believe it's necessary or desirable to display gratitude for something that's clearly defined as the child's duty within the family. "Duties should be done with nothing said," they argue. That attitude won't teach good manners. And it won't teach duties either without some degree of coercion to replace the rejected positive approach. We think that there's *always* a place for gratitude, whether a person is merely doing his duty or going above and beyond it.

Just as Jerry should thank Dad for fixing his bicycle, Dad should thank Jerry for taking out the trash at the appointed time. Each may be performing some responsibility as defined by his general role in the family; each is also entitled to some positive acknowledgment for his contribution.

Remember: A key watchword in all this is "get 'em while they're young!" Very young children are quick to respond to a show of affection and gratitude. You don't have to do much to elicit an infant's smile—a smile from you will do. If you praise a toddler for a simple task, he'll immediately let you know how much you have pleased him—by rewarding you with his own show of pleasure.

As your child gets older, he'll become more and more preoccupied with his surroundings and peer influences, and he may no longer be as responsive to your example. He may take his piece of cake and leave the room abruptly, without so much as a smile of approval or a word of gratitude for his mother's hard work. You gave a service, and you got no reward. "How sharper than a serpent's tooth" is such a response from your child!

In short, when parents are lax about their own manners and also have failed to conduct ongoing, informal lessons about politeness from an early age, they can't expect a mannerly performance from their child. When there is no positive example to follow in the home, the child is apt to consider good manners rather unimportant. Parents, alas, learn to live with it. But outsiders will not have to—they can look elsewhere for friends!

Method 2: "Manners" Negotiation. The second method of teaching children manners is a variation on our old standby, negotiation. In essence, this involves an explicit arrangement to bestow rewards for good conduct.

Here you and your child agree that when the child uses the proper polite terminology to express himself, you will openly and perhaps tangibly express your pleasure for this behavior. This should certainly include a hug, a smile, or words of praise, along with perhaps some more tangible token. Whatever you use, your positive response will go a long way toward building good habits and manners.

How, in practical terms, do you use this method to help bring about a change in your child's approach to everyday courtesies?

As usual, you set up a one-to-one discussion with your youngster. Take her out for a walk or over to the local ice cream shop as a prelude to making your point. Be a loving parent from the start. When the right mood has been established, open up the topic. Tell the child how much it would mean to you for her to be helpful, attentive, and generally well-mannered in the home. Emphasize the growing responsibilities that come with maturity. But remember that these arguments in themselves aren't likely to be persuasive.

One mother and daughter I know struggled with a situation that involved a special kind of courtesy in their particular family setting. The subject in dispute was whether the daughter, Heather, would help her mother carry in the groceries after supermarket trips. The encounters between mother and daughter occurred in four distinct stages, before a negotiated settlement was finally reached.

Stage 1. Mom had just returned from her weekly ordeal at the supermarket. High prices, long lines, and an annoying check-out clerk had made the outing especially unsettling. Just as she began to unload the car—a substantial task, given the six bags of groceries she had accumulated—Heather appeared. Her daughter had just come home from school and was on the way out again.

As the daughter walked out the door wearing her gym togs, the mother asked her to help unload the car. The result was all too predictable. Heather wasn't very willing. Her gymnastics lesson was about to begin, she said, and she had just enough time to walk to the class before it started.

How did Mom handle this situation? Not very well, I'm afraid.

"You're always busy when I want you to help!" the mother exclaimed angrily and tearfully. "I don't see why you can't be a few minutes late so that you can help your poor mother. You ought to pull your weight around here a little more. I do so much for you all the time, and yet when I want a little help myself, you just can't be bothered."

After this heavy dose of guilt, mixed with veiled threats, Heather complied. Why? Not because her mother had persuaded her that parental sacrifices should be repaid. Unfortunately, like most people, Heather simply didn't want to be criticized anymore! She knew that not even escaping to her class would make her mother forget to air her grievances when she got home again.

Obviously this is a negative sort of interaction. In effect, the deal was stated by the mother in unilateral terms this way: "Heather, if you help me, I'm going to stop criticizing you and making you feel guilty. I'll be off your back. It's your duty to help, and I expect you to respond without any complaints. And if you fail to comply, you can see what you're going to get!"

The mother wasn't really aware of what she was doing. But she had learned that tears, anger, and implied threats were a way of getting help when other methods failed. So she naturally took up these tactics when the need arose.

Even though Heather pitched in and helped her mother in this case, she was late for her lesson and her relationship with her mother took a step backward. The mother sensed that she hadn't handled the situation very well; so she decided to try to do a little better during the next stage of their encounters.

Stage 2. Once again, Mom had just returned from a shopping expedition—and again, as if on cue, Heather was just leaving for some important activity. Of course Mom asked Heather to help her unload the car.

But she tried a somewhat different approach this time. Having learned more about negotiating, the mother knew it was important to be more positive and improve her relationship with Heather. So she said gently, "Do you suppose you could help me with this stuff? I'd really appreciate it so that we can get dinner ready on time for your father."

Once more, being the dutiful daughter, Heather helped her mother unload the groceries. Moreover, she didn't complain, at least not immediately. She perhaps realized that unless she complied, Mom's gentle appeal could turn into something else.

But still, Mom and Heather were not getting along too well, not only with groceries but with other household matters. Mom felt Heather should be more helpful—after all, she was fourteen. But it wasn't happening.

Mom's success with her more agreeable form of request made her think more about the concept of negotiation. She realized that despite her expectations of help from Heather, she had no plan to make that help worthwhile for the girl. No wonder she was getting resistance! So Mom decided to see if she could negotiate a solution, beginning with the groceries.

Obviously it's not necessary in a loving family for everything always to "even out" every time one member of the family helps another. But Mom recognized that her shopping expeditions occurred at a time of day when Heather was usually quite busy with her schoolwork or other activities. Anyway, Heather's lack of assistance was being matched by Mom's lack of consideration for whatever help she got.

To work out a satisfactory negotiation in this case, the mother decided to arrange her own schedule for shopping so they would dovetail more with Heather's free time. Then the stage was set for Stage 3 of their interactions.

Stage 3. Despite the adjustments, Heather and her mom found themselves at cross-purposes again after the next shopping trip. The mother again asked Heather to help, but Heather objected—this time she had to study before running off for her gymnastics lesson.

The mother, however, took a step to make the exchange between her and her daughter more equal. "Heather, if you'll please help unload the car for me, I'll drive you to the gym as soon as we're finished," the mother offered.

Now *this* was more like it! At least that was Heather's reaction. Finally she was being tendered a proposition with an adequate benefit. Mom was willing to give up a few minutes of her time in return for Heather's giving up a few minutes and helping with the heavy packages. The girl quickly agreed, and soon they were exchanging services that would benefit both parties about the same.

Stage 4. Now all was ready for the mother to take up Stage 4, a longer-term negotiation. They discussed not only grocery help, but also other chores the mother wanted Heather to assume. Mother and daughter finally realized that services and benefits can be reciprocal. Mutual agreement was the result.

The development of good manners moves us quite naturally to another, equally difficult area of training—the development of good morals. Some will immediately object, "But morals can't be negotiated! If something is right, it's right; if it's wrong, it's wrong. How can this area of conduct be subjected to the principles of bargaining?"

That's a good question and deserves to be dealt with in some depth.

NEGOTIATING MORAL BEHAVIOR

One of the most frequent comments I hear when I discuss negotiation with parents is this: "Moral issues have to be handled in different ways. Moral behavior has to be influenced through spiritual or religious education, not deal making! You can't negotiate about lying or stealing. Don't you agree?"

For many families, religious views form the bedrock for moral education. Even for others, moral training is considered critical. Whatever the source of moral authority, most parents feel a strong need to instruct their children about the importance of distinguishing right from wrong and to act accordingly.

Because the term is used in so many ways, it's not easy to be sure what we're talking about when we refer to "morality." For most people, for example, there is a distinction between morality and social convention. Suppose your daughter insists that she wants to wear huge earrings to school. That raises some questions in your mind, such as, "What will her teachers think? What will other people say?" It may not be clear whether to categorize this issue as moral or as a question of convention. Doing things as others do them is often just fashion, and fashion is hardly morality. So you may not think that your daughter would be doing something immoral or against any basic religious or spiritual values if she wore those earrings. In fact you would have no objection if she wanted wear them to nonschool social functions. But you feel that it's not quite proper for her to wear the earrings to school. Perhaps she just doesn't understand what other people—especially grown-ups—will approve of in youngsters her age.

Or you may take still a different tack. You may feel there are good *moral* reasons to prefer your daughter to dress more modestly. Such an overt display before her peers may offend your religious values in some way.

So is wearing the earrings wrong for moral or merely social reasons? It's not uncommon for people to misunderstand and fail to distinguish between these two possibilities. Finally, though, you'll have to answer such questions yourself, as a parent with your own particular religious and philosophical convictions.

Your moral beliefs may coincide with those of others or they may be quite different. But you may certainly be justified in wanting to pass them on to your offspring—even if they seem somewhat at odds with those of the cultural mainstream.

And some moral principles never seem to change. The ancient Persian fathers were said to have valued three things in their sons: They should be able to ride a horse, shoot an arrow, and tell the truth. We may smile at the first two; they hardly matter in our times. But the last one—truth telling—will certainly strike most people as being as wise today as it was then.

Similarly, in our culture, you'll most likely decide there are definite moral implications involved in such questions as:

- What should be my child's approach to sex before marriage?
- What about cheating on homework or exams?
- What about using profane or obscene language?
- What about being generous to those who are needy?
- What about stealing and lying?

It's important to come to some definite conclusions about the moral principles involved in these and other questions before you even consider trying to talk to your child about them, or trying to establish rules for his behavior. You have to make up your own mind about morality before you try to help your child make up his. If you think about your own rules, you may find there's a considerable difference between what you might say in the abstract to a child and what you actually regard as acceptable in a specific instance. Circumstances alter cases, as all lawyers and judges know.

But once you've more or less settled these questions in your own mind, you're ready to deal with the next question: "Can negotiation have a role in helping develop my child's moral behavior?"

I believe the answer is emphatically *yes!* Perhaps negotiation can't be the be-all and end-all of moral instruction. But it *can* be an extremely useful tool.

To understand how negotiation and morality can mesh, consider for a moment how moral development takes place. Usually we expose our children directly to the great teachings of religion and philosophy. Not only that, we may go into considerable detail at home, describing the practical applications of morality and the implications of moral and immoral behavior.

But discussion alone won't provide a sufficient incentive for a child to incorporate morality and spirituality into his daily life. So in teaching morality to youngsters, we must rely on explaining the meaning of individual examples in the child's experience. Some of those examples will center on how the child failed to meet moral demands. But if the parent is wise, he'll praise the child when he has acted properly.

Here we come back to the old question of sanctions and rewards. It isn't enough to say, "Johnny, it's important for you to behave this way because that's what a good boy should do. Besides, if you do you'll become a happier, better-adjusted adult." The benefits of following the moral action may well not be concrete or immediate enough to impress the child. Moreover, a simple statement of what is correct to do isn't sufficient to overcome the immediate pressure to act otherwise.

Most parents therefore fall back on various forms of coercion or punishment to enforce moral behavior. They'll respond, "You cheated, so you're going to get a spanking!" Or, "You should apologize to that little girl over there for bullying her, and until you do you'll not get any special favors—including dinner—from me!"

This may not quite be a fire-and-brimstone method of enforcing morality, but it does tend to highlight the negatives rather than the positives of good moral behavior. In fact, in many children, especially older ones, this approach may provoke a reaction opposite to what you want. Instead of stopping her cheating or bullying, your daughter may begin to engage in more of those very things as an expression of rebellion.

In this regard, I'm reminded of an often overlooked passage in the Bible, where St. Paul says, "Fathers, do not provoke your children to anger . . ." (Ephesians 6:4, Revised Standard Version). Instruction and even discipline can be important in developing a moral sense, but punishment can provoke rather than persuade. Negotiation, on the other hand, can open the way to a satisfying solution.

To illustrate how this works, let's consider an example involving a particular point of morality—lying. Kim, a nine-year-old, had gotten into the habit of telling occasional fibs, especially when she found herself in a position in which she was afraid she might be reprimanded or punished.

On one occasion when she was younger, she was asked by her mother, "Did you throw that sand into Mary's hair?"

From the accusing tone of her mother's voice, Kim suspected that she had done something very, very wrong, and that the truth might not be rewarding. So she denied it: "No, no, I didn't do it."

Of course, she *had* done it, and before the day was out, Kim's mother learned the truth of the matter. "Why did you lie to me?" the mother asked.

"Because I thought you'd get mad and punish me," the girl replied honestly.

"Well, I *am* going to punish you," the mother replied. "I want you to go to your room right after supper. You won't get to watch any television or be with the family tonight."

In this case, the mother thought that the punishment would act as a deterrent to Kim's lying in the future. But instead the girl became more adept at fibbing. She learned how to cover her tracks a little better, and many times she managed to escape detection.

But not always.

When her mother did catch Kim in telling lies, she was particularly disturbed by the obvious fact that the girl was so skillful at formulating falsehoods. Sometimes she would answer her mother in a way that could be interpreted either as a lie or perhaps as a slight "shading" of the truth. In those circumstances it was sometimes hard for the mother to establish whether the girl had told a clear-cut fib or not.

Aware that Kim was deeply involved in a practice that the family standards held to be immoral, as well as socially disgraceful, the mother realized that another tack was necessary. She would have to take some approach other than simply punishing the girl every time she caught her.

The mother decided to try some negotiating to resolve the problem. This family happened to be quite religious, and the girl went to religious services regularly. She had been taught that the Bible should be authoritative in her life. So the mother devised an approach to the lying problem that combined both the love and respect that the parents had tried to foster in the family and the spiritual values the girl had been taught.

The mother sat down with the girl in a quiet, pleasant setting—a peaceful neighborhood park late on a Saturday morning—and opened a conversation about the matter. "You know, I'm concerned that sometimes you don't quite tell the truth about things," the mother began, "and I'd like for us to talk about that a little bit." Then she mentioned a couple of instances in which Kim had been caught in an outright lie or had bent the truth to a noticeable extent.

Predictably the girl was defensive. But the mother carefully avoided any direct accusations because she already knew that that approach, along with punishment, hadn't worked very well in the past. Also, she emphasized how much she disliked imposing sanctions and how she'd like to find a better way.

Finally the girl admitted that she lied sometimes, and that provided a real opening in the conversation. The mother replied: "I'm worried about what lying is going to do to your relationships with other people. Others will stop trusting you if they sense that you may not keep your word or you may tell a fib. Your friends, in particular, will begin to get that feeling about you. They may not even want to be your friends anymore."

This argument was familiar to the girl from previous discussions and lectures, but it seemed to make some impression—though it wasn't a decisive point. So the mother pushed on to her next argument: "Also, it's important for us as parents to know that you're doing the right thing, the thing that we've taught you is the proper and moral thing to do. We'll love you in any case. But we're very, very pleased when you do what's right. And it hurts us when you do what's wrong."

At this point, the mother's loving manner touched the daughter. They both shed a tear or two. One of the main reasons Kim had begun lying in the first place was to avoid her parents' disapproval. But the mother's personal feelings of pain about her lying were something she hadn't understood before.

"And there's another thing," her mother continued. "You've been going to church for many years. You know what the Bible says about lying. God is very pleased when you tell the truth, no matter what the consequences may be to you. You may get by with telling a lie sometimes when human beings like your father and I are involved. But when it comes to God, He always knows what you're doing and thinking."

Appeals like this can be very persuasive and effective with children in religious homes. Kim had not yet developed a full perspective on how her habit of lying fit into the morality of her family and her faith. It was extremely important to point out these factors to her because she wanted to please her family and her God.

Kim agreed with her mother that she would tell the truth, even when it hurt. But the mother recognized that her daughter's lying had become too deeply ingrained to have been eliminated by their talk together, no matter how heart-felt their agreement seemed to have been. Therefore the mother agreed that she would try to recognize Kim's efforts toward greater truthfulness; when Kim had clearly resisted a temptation toward falsehood, she would reward Kim tangibly. They decided not to make a specific arrangement for future occasions that would be so hard to predict. But the mother promised that she would try to offset whatever cost Kim's truthfulness might have for her. The mother felt that Kim would eventually learn the advantages of a reputation for honesty, and this arrangement should help her to do so.

Kim's tendency to lie gradually decreased, and the parents were quite happy with this development. But Kim did occasionally meet challenges at school that were too much for her. Taking her school-owned clarinet home for practice one day, she left it in a restaurant. When she went back to look for it, the clarinet was gone.

Ashamed of her forgetfulness and afraid of what her not

very friendly music teacher would say, she lied. She said she knew nothing about the clarinet's disappearance, but the teacher had reason to wonder about her story. Another student had seen Kim carrying the clarinet away from school the evening it was lost, and not wanting to be blamed himself, he informed the teacher. The teacher didn't know which student to believe.

Meanwhile Kim began to feel guilty about what she had done, and she became fearful of punishment, both for the loss of the clarinet and for her lie. She eventually revealed the truth to her mother and asked for forgiveness and help.

The mother saw this as a good opportunity for moral instruction and for relying on their negotiated agreement, and she responded wisely. Although the family would have to pay for the clarinet, the mother felt Kim's truthfulness more than made up for the loss.

"You kept your agreement with me," she said. "You've told the truth, and I'll do everything I can to see that the school doesn't punish you. You'll have to apologize to your music teacher, though. If she does punish you, remember that you have our backing and love. And we'll cover the cost of replacing the instrument."

The mother knew that Kim's fears of punishment at school were greatly exaggerated, and her evaluation of the situation proved correct. The final result was that Kim's apology to the teacher was a rewarding experience for her.

Afterward Kim's mother praised the girl for the way she had finally decided to act. Despite the initial lie, which was certainly a fault, Kim had done the right thing by later being truthful, the mother explained. She had fulfilled her agreement not to lie to her mom, and in return the mother helped to reduce the seriousness of Kim's behavior for her as much as she could.

Her reward for Kim was more than praise and approval, however. It involved direct action to relieve whatever punishment the school might exact for the loss of the clarinet.

Effective moral training often follows the course described in the case of Kim and her mom. We give children guidance through examples and direct instruction. We also make it clear that following the instructed path will meet with the approval of honorable people, and—depending on the religious orientation of the home—of a higher power above. Like other disciplinary practices, however, moral training generally also includes references to the disastrous effects of disapproved behavior. Both love and fear are evoked, with promises of prosperity or misery, either in this life or the next.

Parents, ministers, priests, or rabbis all act so as to reinforce or punish the child who conforms to or deviates from the ideal. Thus for training in moral behavior, just as for other behavior, the use of reward and punishment is commonplace. Here we are advocating nothing novel. We only want to emphasize what can be done with the positive approach when it's conducted in an informed way.

With questions of morality, it's also important for you to be a good role model. For example, suppose you want to encourage your child to help the needy. If your youngster sees you giving things away to those less fortunate, he's more likely to follow suit. But when the child gives, those gifts need not be the youngster's favorite toys. The pleasure of the recipient can come across to the child as a reward unconnected with any pain or loss on the part of the child. Later the child will most likely willingly part even with goods valuable to himself as well as to the receiver.

It's also helpful if the act of giving can be surrounded by excitement and fun. Try, for example, praising, patting, and smiling at an infant for offering a bit of his breakfast cereal to someone. Usually you'll find he'll happily give it all away!

One family I know began to get their young son into the habit of helping the homeless in one large American city by turning the event into a family outing. They all went down to a local soup kitchen, rolled up their sleeves, and made sandwiches and prepared other food for some of the hungry people in the neighborhood. Then they participated in handing out the food to some of the patrons of the kitchen and engaged them in conversation.

All the while, the ten-year-old child in the family was not only observing what his parents were doing but also participating. The boy helped to pack sandwiches in paper bags and contributed some of his allowance to the kitty that was used to buy the food. He met some of the other helpers, and they told him interesting stories about their work. As a result, he got the impression that giving his time and money to help others didn't simply mean depriving himself of something. He learned that reaching out to others could be enjoyable and adventurous as well.

By using such an approach, you're much more likely to encourage your child to embark on a course of moral behavior that will *stick*—not one that will fade away when you're not around to monitor his conduct.

An important objective of teaching morality is to encourage behavior that will persist even when there is little or no threat that a person's lapses will be detected. The ultimate test of moral strength, many people feel, is persistence in a moral line of action in an unrewarding or even punishing environment. And there are ways you can instill such behavior in your children.

For example, if you feel that it's important to be honest, then you should be honest when a grocery clerk unwittingly hands you a quarter too much in change—and you're the only one who knows it. As a conscientious, consistent person, you acknowledge that giving back the quarter is the only right thing to do. Furthermore, you'd like your children to have this built-in moral sense as well.

At first, it may seem that neither rewards nor punishments can produce such morality. But that really isn't so. Here's a simple way such behavior develops. I call it the cookie-crumb theory of moral behavior. One day your little Nancy enters the kitchen and discovers that no one is in sight. A cookie jar is sitting on the counter, full of tempting chocolate chip cookies, and Nancy simply can't restrain herself. Although she knows she is not supposed to have one before dinner, she decides to take the risk: She looks around, sees no one is near, and sneaks three of those cookies from the jar.

Nancy isn't old enough to realize that the cookie crumbs she's dropped on the floor are sure evidence that someone has eaten some of those cookies. When Mom questions her about the missing cookies, Nancy feels perfectly safe in lying. She says, "I didn't take any."

But because there are no other suspects and the crumbs were right there on the counter, Mom knows that she's hearing a lie. So she confronts Nancy for not telling the truth.

In this case, Nancy was not experienced enough to see that she would be caught by the traces she left after her theft. She saw no way that her secret transgression would be detected. But still, for reasons she couldn't fathom, she *was* caught!

What are the implications of such experiences?

Obviously, this cookie-crumb example has little to do with negotiation. Still Nancy has learned that lying carries with it unpleasant consequences. She also learned that she is frequently caught, even when it seems to her that no one can detect what she has done. Her ensuing honesty is not based on her own fine judgments about whether or not someone is giving to punish her behavior. Instead, because her judgments often turn out wrong, her honesty becomes more automatic than thought-out.

As Nancy grows older, other temptations will come her way, and a more sophisticated approach to moral instruction will be necessary. But it's good for a very young child to learn that the world is a complicated place and that trying to judge in a self-serving way whether or not a moral infraction will succeed isn't very wise.

Beginning moral training early can reinforce the inclination not to make moral decisions on self-serving grounds. For example, when your child, as an adult, gets too much change from a cashier, she will *know* that she is extremely unlikely to be detected if she keeps the money. Perhaps she can even rationalize her actions by telling herself how often cashiers have overcharged her at other times. But the more deeply ingrained her moral actions have become from an early age, the less likely she is to choose the dishonest route.

There are intangible benefits that accrue to those who behave with integrity and uprightness. On the simplest level, your child will probably feel a rush of pleasure as she smiles and returns the undeserved change. And that pleasure won't arise from relief at not being punished for being dishonest. More likely she'll be remembering the satisfaction she derived from parental approval for truthful and honest actions in the "little things" of the past.

10.

The Great Goal of Self-Control

*N*EGOTIATING with kids should never be an end in itself.

Behind all parent-child negotiating there should be the ultimate goal of teaching a child self-control and personal discipline. These qualities will help the youngster become a self-starter who can operate well in life without constant parental supervision.

The most effective negotiations will lead to the child's greater sense of independence and personal responsibility. And the youngster will develop important verbal and reasoning skills during the process that will be invaluable as he confronts the challenges of later life.

But the process has to start in small ways and should begin at young ages. One mother and daughter began to run into problems because the girl, an extremely active and intelligent ten-year-old, refused to make her bed regularly. It's not quite accurate to say that she "refused." More often she simply "forgot." She always seemed to have more important things on her mind.

Finally the mother decided to open negotiations on this subject, and the two of them quickly agreed on terms. According to the arrangement, the girl would receive an increase in her allowance each week for making her bed during that week.

But she would get that increase in increments, equally divided among the seven days of each week. And to make the rewards immediate, the mother gave the girl a token—a poker chip representing the extra money—*each day,* as she earned it. So if she made her bed all seven days of a given week, she would get seven tokens that she could exchange for the complete increase in her allowance at the end of that week. On the other hand, if she only made her bed five days in a week, she would get five-sevenths of the additional allowance.

During the first few weeks, the parent monitored the girl's progress each day. The mother would stick her head in the door each morning before the girl left for school and say something like: "Bed all made up?" No nagging. No coaxing or pleading. Just a quick, one-shot reminder. Then the token would be given to indicate the portion of allowance that had been earned.

After the bed-making procedure was firmly in place for a few weeks, the mother began to decrease her monitoring. For one thing, she quit issuing those reminders. Instead she just checked to see that the bed had been made after the child had left for school. The mother was testing whether the girl could continue her bed making even if there was no *immediate* praise or reminder. She also replaced the token award with check marks on a sheet of paper attached to the refrigerator door. Her daughter could examine this sheet whenever she came home from school.

Things went along fairly well on this basis for a while. So the mother took another step to disengage herself from any involvement in the bed-making process. First she began to give the girl her rewards on a cumulative basis. She inspected quietly every day, but she gave a check mark only every two days. Then she shifted to check marks every three or four days; and finally she began to give check marks at the end of each week, along with the regular allowance payment. The rewards remained the same—one seventh of the extra allowance for each day's bed making. But the child had to work all week with no feedback from the mother.

Consider what had happened: At first the goal had been to make the bed once, with an immediate consequence to follow. Now the goal was to make the bed daily for long periods, with no consequence at all from the parents, except for the weekly check marks and extra money.

On a gradual, step-by-step basis, the mother began to give her daughter more control over this part of her life. When they started out, the mother's constant, almost hovering presence had been necessary to establish the basic habit. Once the daughter had shown she could perform well with close supervision, she was given more leeway.

Finally this ten-year-old developed a significant degree of self-control over one small but important task at home—keeping her bed in order. With a little hinting from Mom, the girl said she didn't need the check-mark system at all anymore. So her mother began to give her the increase in her allowance without reference to the bed making. The mother still checked now and then just to see that all was going along well.

This simple example demonstrates the ultimate goal of every attempted negotiation. You as a parent want to design the negotiating process so that less and less close supervision and fewer rewards are needed in the areas of conduct that have been at issue. Ultimately you should to be able to step back and allow your child to operate on his own; as he becomes independent of your control he gains more power over his own life. Of course other people will continue to influence his behavior, but that is as it should and must be. It's your parental management that must diminish.

A major ingredient of self-control is the ability for the child to be goal-oriented—and to *achieve* those goals once they've been set. In part this quality involves an ability on the part of the child to set goals farther and farther in the future and to work toward them steadily until they have been accomplished. As children grow older, they express their self-control by developing a broader, more comprehensive understanding and use of time in their lives.

One example of this involved a six-year-old boy who managed to set a goal two months in the future and then work on an almost daily basis to achieve it. This accomplishment was rather remarkable in light of the child's age, but the basic principles involved say a lot to any parents who are attempting to develop self-control and independence in their children.

The boy and his father had been involved in negotiating on a relatively small scale for a year or so. One of the things they started out with was exercise. The youngster had been having a few health problems, and the father suspected that the source of the difficulty lay in the child's lack of regular activity. So he devised a system whereby the boy would get regular rewards, equal to the cost of the bus fare, if he walked or ran to school each morning.

When they began this program, there were a number of rough places in working out the system. At first the father accompanied the boy, who resisted the running segments of the trip. "I get too tired, Daddy!" he would say. So the father found himself in the midst of regular renegotiations on the way to school each morning. He periodically reduced the length and number of running segments until the breathless complaints from the youngster came less often.

Still the bus fare at the end of the trip—and the opportunity to be with his father for an extra twenty-five minutes each day—were enough to keep this boy going. Interestingly the youngster's health problems decreased markedly after he had embarked on this program. His running ability, of course, greatly increased, and the agreement was renegotiated for more jogging and less walking.

Even more interesting for our purposes, the boy came to *expect* to walk and run to school each morning. Soon he and his father actually forgot about the payment of the reward. They both ran all the way, and then the father left his happy son at school and went on about his day. Shortly afterward he was able to send the boy off alone.

What we see here is the development of a discipline that required less and less pushing and supervision on the part of the parent. The activity that at first had to be rewarded had come to be pleasurable in itself—and needed no external encouragement. The boy actually began to enjoy his morning's vigorous exercise. So at least up to this point, it seems that the negotiating process had helped him take some giant steps toward greater self-control.

But this is just the first part of the story.

The same youngster, now ten years old, had engaged in many further negotiating sessions with his father, and eventually he was ready for a more significant test. The occasion arose when the boy decided that he wanted a toy train set that cost slightly more than one hundred dollars.

First he tried the usual approach that most children use. He asked his parents to buy it for him. But he got a solid set of refusals: "No, that costs way too much for us right now. And you've got too many toys as it is!"

But then the father, remembering all those sessions of negotiating, threw out another possibility: "Maybe you could earn it."

The boy, with considerable experience at earning rewards behind him, immediately responded, "Okay."

What remained was for the two of them to work out a system of rewards that would allow the youngster to accumulate enough money to buy the train. The boy had already earned about forty dollars. Since the train set cost one hundred ten dollars, the father proposed, "If you'll earn sixty dollars more and add that to the forty dollars you already have, your mother and I will make up the difference."

The boy immediately accepted and then proposed tasks that he would have to perform in order to earn the required amount. He came up with a variety of possibilities: taking care of his laundry, helping his father keep the car sparkling, playing his violin without complaining for the required amount of time, and a number of other behaviors that he knew the parents wanted to encourage. Finally he wrote out a contract that his parents agreed to sign, errors and all.

Both the mother and father expected that the boy would lose interest after a few days and that the toy would be forgotten in short order. But the youngster stuck to his goal like a bulldog.

He stayed motivated in part because he had posted a large picture of the train in his room. So he had a graphic reminder of his goal constantly in front of him. This train set could be expanded and integrated into a larger system, and he could foresee a larger and larger railway system coming into being in his basement playroom. He stuck to his ambition for two months, and at the end of that time, he had earned an additional sixty dollars from doing his various tasks—enough to make his purchase and achieve his goal.

The family organized a special outing to buy the train and bring it home. The boy led the way like a conquering hero! How mature he looked, so confident and self-possessed, his parents thought, as they followed along. And all this had happened as a result of negotiations he had conducted on his own.

As your child's self-control and self-discipline grow and expand, so will his sense of independence and power. If you pursue the negotiating process on a regular basis, you'll find it less and less necessary to supervise and monitor his progress and activities.

The values that you have chosen to impart to him through various deals will become a deeply ingrained part of his being. Soon he'll create his own goals, establish a strategy to reach them, and then move steadily toward the accomplishment of those objectives. He'll be well on his way toward becoming an adult—the mature and competent adult you hope for.

Reservations may occur to you as this process is taking place. You want very much to see your child develop and mature into an independent self-starter. But as that begins to happen, you may sense that you're losing control too quickly. You may worry that your "little one" is growing too fast and soon you'll be left with an empty nest. That's always a sad prospect in one respect because there can be so many happy moments in caring for a young child. But keep in mind that your child's maturity and progress are your ultimate goals. If he didn't develop into an independent, highly motivated adult, you would undoubtedly feel that in some way you had failed.

So brace yourself for the time when your offspring spreads her wings and flies the coop! Concentrate on developing those negotiating skills and give your youngsters plenty of opportunity to grow. Then you'll see them become more and more persuasive and forceful with you, as they make unanswerable points and move the grounds of discussions around to their best advantage. You'll also be less likely to see them leave without a glance behind, or with the memories of harsh and unforgiving words and deeds grating on their minds.

Can it be threatening to a parent when he finds himself outreasoned by his child? You bet it can! But even as you feel a little disconcerted, or threatened, keep the big picture in mind. You haven't been bested by your child. Rather you've done an excellent job of transferring important family and personal values to a malleable young mind. You've shaped the future of a son or daughter who will be admirably equipped not only to take on Mom and Dad, but also the toughest challenges from the outside world.

Selected Bibliography

Axelrod, S., and Apsche, J. *The Effects of Punishment on Human Behavior.* New York: Academic Press, 1982. A scholarly book surveying the extensive research on punishment and its effects on children. Includes chapters on the use of time out, social reprimands, side effects of punishment, and ethical and legal issues.

Blechman, E. A. *Solving Child Behavior Problems at Home and at School.* Champaign, Ill.: Research Press, 1986. Includes a training program to teach children and parents cooperation in mutual problem solving, for problems such as fighting, lying, disobedience.

Fisher, R., and Ury, W. *Getting to Yes.* Boston: Houghton-Mifflin Co., 1981. A classic book on negotiating without hostility and without giving in. Written for parents and anyone else concerned about their skills as negotiators.

The following four references are booklets, all written in simple language and designed to form a set.

Hall, R. V., and Hall, M. C. *How to Use Time Out.* H & H Enterprises, Inc., Box 1070-E, Lawrence, Kan. 66044. A simple how-to book with clear language and many real-life examples of what to do, and what to do when that doesn't work.

———*How to Use Planned Ignoring.* H & H Enterprises (address above). Not paying attention to your child, at the right times, can be the best thing that ever happened to you. But you must learn how to do it.

How to Use Systematic Attention and Approval. H & H Enterprises (address above). Particularly useful if you feel you have to attend too much to your child. How to use attention and shows of love for creative purposes.

Hall, R.V., and Van Houten, R. *How to Use Reprimands.* H & H Enterprises (address above). Particularly useful for parents who find that their efforts to discipline their children involve too many ineffective reprimands.

Kosloff, M. A. *A Program for Families of Children with Learning and Behavior Problems.* New York: Wiley-Interscience. A guide for trainers of parents and teachers, to help them overcome problems with their children; but parents themselves can use it. A step-by-step fifteen-part program.

Morris, R. J., and Kratochwill, T. R. *Treating Children's Fears and Phobias.* Elmsford, N.Y.: Pergamon Press, 1982. A report of research on the problem of children's fears—from mild to serious. Not written especially for parents, but full of case studies and detailed descriptions of fear-reduction methods.

Patterson, G. R. *Families.* Champaign, Ill.: Research Press, 1975. Written for parents, to help them change the way they manage their children and the ways their children manage them. Deals with such problems as whining, temper tantrums, aggression, stealing.

Pumroy, D. K., and Pumroy, S. S. *Modern Childrearing.* Chicago: Nelson-Hall, 1978. A practical guide, written at a more advanced level, for undergraduate student instruction—but also useful for parents. Includes some basic research studies that have led to the development of modern parenting methods.

Strayhorn, J. M. *Talking It Out.* Champaign, Ill., Research Press, 1977. Constructive ways to resolve conflicts. Teaches you to identify the messages you are sending along with the actual words you use; with many examples and exercises.

Wagonseller, B. R., and McDowell, R. L. *You and Your Child.* Champaign, Ill.,: Research Press,. 1979. For parents, advice that encourages the view that parents and children are a team, not rivals for power.

Warschaw, T. A. *Winning by Negotiation.* New York: McGraw-Hill, 1980. How to negotiate, with examples from personal relations, business, and the home, with a brief section on children. Emphasis on tactics, how to recognize what tactics you are using, and how to use tactics successfully.